A-LEVEL YEAR 2
STUDENT GUIDE

AQA

Physics

Options 9 and 12

Astrophysics

Turning points in physics

Jeremy Pollard

HODDER
EDUCATION
AN HACHETTE UK COMPANY

Hodder Education, an Hachette UK company, Blenheim Court, George Street, Banbury, Oxfordshire OX16 5BH

Orders

Bookpoint Ltd, 130 Park Drive, Milton Park, Abingdon, Oxfordshire OX14 4SE

tel: 01235 827827

fax: 01235 400401

e-mail: education@bookpoint.co.uk

Lines are open 9.00 a.m.–5.00 p.m., Monday to Saturday, with a 24-hour message answering service. You can also order through the Hodder Education website: www.hoddereducation.co.uk

© Jeremy Pollard 2016

ISBN 978-1-4718-5912-0

First printed 2016

Impression number 5 4 3 2 1

Year 2020 2019 2018 2017 2016

This guide has been written specifically to support students preparing for the AQA A-level Physics examinations. The content has been neither approved nor endorsed by AQA and remains the sole responsibility of the author.

Cover photo: Beboy/Fotolia; Figure 20 Jeremy Pollard

Typeset by Integra Software Services Pvt. Ltd., Pondicherry, India

Printed in Italy

Hachette UK's policy is to use papers that are natural, renewable and recyclable products and made from wood grown in sustainable forests. The logging and manufacturing processes are expected to conform to the environmental regulations of the country of origin.

Contents

Content Guidance

Astrophysics

Turning points in physics

Questions & Answers

■ Getting the most from this book

Exam-style questions

Sample student answers

Practise the questions, then look at the student answers that follow.

Commentary on sample student answers

Read the comments (preceded by the icon ⓔ) showing how many marks each answer would be awarded in the exam and exactly where marks are gained or lost.

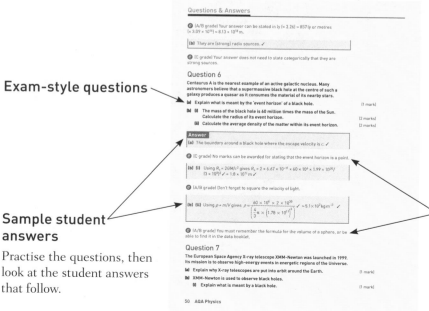

About this book

This guide covers two of the optional sections — 'Astrophysics' and 'Turning points in physics' — of the A-level specification for AQA Physics. It is intended to help you to remember and understand the physics you need for the course and is set out in the same order as the specification so that you can check that you have covered everything. There are two main sections:

- The **Content Guidance** covers the main points of the topics. It is not a detailed textbook — it is intended to help you understand what is needed and how to use that understanding and knowledge in questions. The worked examples should help you to understand the principles and to see the sorts of questions that you might be required to undertake in an examination. There are some quick knowledge check questions that will help you to be sure you understand each physics point. Answers are given at the end of the book.

- The **Questions & Answers** section contains two test papers with answers, so that you can practise questions and see the sorts of answers that are needed, along with the knowledge and understanding required.

You will need to learn the basic facts and ensure that you understand the connections between different ideas. It is often helpful to learn beyond the specification so that these connections become more obvious. The more you can do that, the better you will be able to tackle new questions or different ideas. If you try all the questions in this book and more besides you will be able to approach any examination with confidence.

Content Guidance

■ Astrophysics

Astrophysics is the study of the Universe. You need to know how telescopes are used to gather information about cosmological objects, such as stars and exoplanets, and how fundamental physics principles are used to analyse and explain their behaviour. You also need to know about the principles of operation of telescopes.

Telescopes

Observational astronomy involves the use of telescopes to capture electromagnetic radiation emitted by objects in space. There are two main types of telescope — refracting telescopes (using lenses) and reflecting telescopes (involving mirrors).

Refracting astronomical telescopes

Refracting telescopes use lenses and the principle of refraction of electromagnetic waves to form an image. Glass lenses are generally used to study the visible light emitted by objects, and two lenses (a long focal length objective lens and a short focal length eyepiece) are needed to observe distant objects in space. Rays of light coming from distant objects, such as the stars in an open cluster, arrive in parallel at the objective lens. In **normal adjustment** (of objects such as stars) the objective lens forms an intermediate image within the telescope and the eyepiece then forms a magnified virtual image of the intermediate image that is observed by the eye, as shown in Figure 1.

A telescope is in **normal adjustment** if the object that it is observing is effectively an infinite distance away from the telescope.

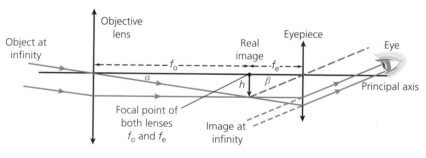

Figure 1 A refracting astronomical telescope

The angular magnification, M, of a refracting telescope in normal adjustment is given by:

$$M = \frac{\text{angle subtended by the image at eye}}{\text{angle subtended by the object at unaided eye}} = \frac{f_o}{f_e}$$

where f_o is the **focal length** of the objective lens and f_e is the focal length of the eyepiece lens.

The **focal length** of a convex converging lens is the distance from the centre of the lens to the focal point of the lens, as shown in Figure 2.

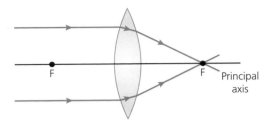

Figure 2 Rays parallel to the principal axis meet at the focal point

Reflecting telescopes

The vast majority of large telescopes in the world are reflecting telescopes. There are a variety of different arrangements of the two main mirrors needed to form an observable image by eye. One of the most popular arrangements of the mirrors is used in the Cassegrain reflecting telescope, as shown in Figure 3.

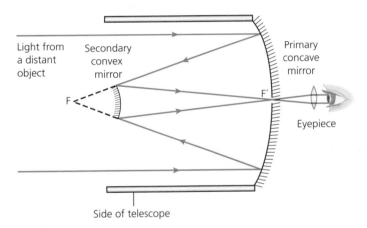

Figure 3 Principle of the Cassegrain reflecting telescope

This arrangement is popular because the telescope tube can be made quite short, but a large primary concave parabolic mirror can still be used — increasing the amount of light that is captured by the telescope. The primary mirror reflects the light to a focal point at F, but a small convex secondary mirror mounted inside the telescope tube reflects the light back through a small hole in the primary mirror placed at the focal point F′. This arrangement has a second advantage — the observer views the image in the same direction as the telescope is pointing, allowing easier alignment with the object being observed.

Exam tip

The ability of a telescope to collect light is called its 'collecting power' and is proportional to the square of the diameter (and hence area) of the aperture of the telescope. A bigger aperture allows more light to be collected and so fainter objects can be imaged.

Knowledge check 1

A refracting telescope has an objective lens with a focal length of 120 cm, and an eyepiece with a focal length of 15 mm. Calculate the angular magnification of the telescope.

Exam tip

Astronomical telescopes act as 'light buckets' increasing the amount of light entering the eye. The objects being imaged appear brighter and more spread out, i.e. magnified in angle.

Reflectors v refractors (mirrors v lenses)

Table 1 summarises the advantages of each type of telescope.

Table 1

Advantages of reflectors	Advantages of refractors
It is much easier to manufacture and support large-diameter mirrors than large-diameter lenses.	Large refractors have sealed tubes and require little maintenance. The reflective coating of large mirror surfaces open to the air may need periodic recoating.
Mirrors do not suffer from **chromatic aberration**, where light of different colours is refracted along different paths, forming a range of different focal points, blurring the image, as shown in Figure 4. 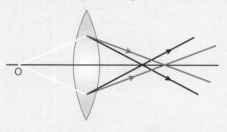 **Figure 4** Chromatic aberration produced by a lens	The lenses in refractors are held firmly in position by the tube. The mirrors in a reflector sometimes move out of position and need realignment.
Curved mirrors suffer far less from **spherical aberration**, in which rays of light coming from different parts of the lens (or mirror) go to slightly different focal points because the lens or mirror is not a perfect shape, as shown in Figure 5. The curved mirrors inside a reflecting telescope are parabolic in shape and focus the rays of light parallel to the principal axis to a sharp focal point reducing blurring. 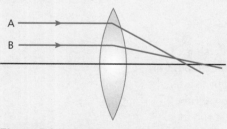 **Figure 5** Spherical aberration produced by a lens	The small secondary mirror inside a reflector blocks some of the light from entering the imaging system. Refractors do not have this problem.
Very large mirrors can be made and supported easily by the telescope mount. The Gran Telescopio on La Palma has a diameter of 10.4 m. Large lenses sag under their own weight and require immense supports. The Yerkes telescope in Wisconsin is only 1.02 m in diameter.	The secondary mirror inside a reflector and its supports cause some diffraction of the light, blurring the image slightly. Refractors do not have this problem.

Chromatic aberration occurs where light of different colours are refracted along different paths, forming a range of different focal points, blurring the image.

Spherical aberration occurs where rays of light coming from different parts of the lens (or mirror) go to slightly different focal points due to the lens or mirror being out of (the correct) shape.

Exam tip

Comparison of the advantages (or disadvantages) of reflecting and refracting telescopes is a common examination question. Make sure that you learn the advantages of both.

Knowledge check 2

What is meant by **(a)** spherical aberration and **(b)** chromatic aberration?

Knowledge check 3

Explain why a reflecting telescope will not suffer from chromatic aberration, whereas a refracting telescope will.

Advantages of large-diameter telescopes

The **resolving power** of an astronomical telescope is dictated by its ability to *just* resolve (see) two objects very close together in the night sky as distinct objects. Larger telescopes have much better resolving powers than smaller diameter telescopes. Resolving power is given as an angle θ (measured in radians) by the Rayleigh criterion:

$$\theta \approx \frac{\lambda}{D}$$

where λ is the wavelength of the light from the object (measured in metres) and D is the diameter of the aperture of the telescope (measured in metres). The Rayleigh criterion defines the angle between two objects where the first diffraction minimum of one object occurs at the same angle as the central maximum of the second object, as shown in Figure 6.

The **resolving power** of a telescope is the minimum angular separation of two objects in space that can be imaged as distinct sources — it is given by the Rayleigh criterion.

(a)   **(b)**   **(c)**

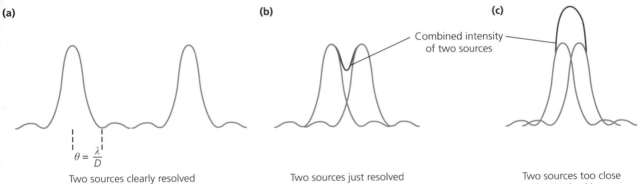

Combined intensity of two sources

$\theta = \frac{\lambda}{D}$

Two sources clearly resolved   Two sources just resolved by the Raleigh criterion   Two sources too close to be resolved by eye

Figure 6 Principle of the Rayleigh criterion

The ability of a telescope system to image objects clearly is also dictated by the detection system used to form the image. This is related to the resolution and quantum efficiency of the detector. Modern imaging systems use **charge-coupled devices** (CCDs) to produce an electronic image that can be stored or displayed digitally. These are the same electronic chips that are used to form images in digital cameras and camera phones. The resolution of a CCD is nearly always given in megapixels (the number of light sensitive pixels present on the chip) and more pixels produce a higher resolution. The quantum efficiency (usually expressed as a percentage) is the proportion of incoming photons from the object that are converted into electrons as the detector signal:

$$\text{quantum efficiency} = \frac{\text{number of electrons produced per second}}{\text{number of photons absorbed per second}}$$

Table 2 compares the resolution and quantum efficiency of the human eye with a large telescope CCD chip.

A **charge-coupled device (CCD)** is an electronic light detector, commonly used in electronic cameras, phones and tablets.

Knowledge check 4

Calculate the resolving power of a 32 cm diameter reflecting telescope primary mirror imaging light with a wavelength of 620 nm.

Exam tip

You do not need to know the structure of a CCD imaging chip.

Table 2

Device	Resolution	Quantum efficiency (%)
Human eye	574 megapixels (equivalent)	1–4
CCD chip	1400 megapixels	70–90

Radio, infrared, ultraviolet and X-ray telescopes

Radio telescopes

Radio signals from objects in space can be usefully observed on Earth between the wavelengths of 30 cm and about 3 m (compared to about 400 to 700 nm for light). This means that radio telescopes need large **apertures**, and because the radio signals coming from objects in space are incredibly weak, the larger the dish the higher the collecting power.

All large radio telescopes are reflectors (like most large optical telescopes) and, because most radio signals pass unhindered through the atmosphere, there is a much wider range of potential sites for professional radio astronomy, compared to professional optical telescopes that tend to be situated in high, dry locations — for example on the summit of mountains like Mauna Kea in Hawaii. Radio telescopes can be extremely large, and can be made even larger by combining several together. The 305 m diameter Arecibo radio telescope, built into a valley in the hills of Puerto Rico, is 30 times larger than the 10 m Gran Telescopio on La Palma.

Radio telescopes tend to be used to image some of the most energetic physical processes in the Universe, but they have much lower resolving powers than optical telescopes. A 1 m optical telescope has a resolving power of 0.3 arcseconds, compared to 30 arcminutes for a large radio telescope — about 6000 times lower resolution.

Infrared and ultraviolet telescopes

Infrared (IR) and ultraviolet (UV) telescopes have similar construction and operation to optical telescopes, because their wavelengths are at either end of the optical spectrum. The Earth's atmosphere absorbs most of the UV radiation that hits the Earth, so all UV telescopes are space-based, sited onboard satellites. Some IR radiation penetrates the atmosphere and several of the large professional telescope observatories have IR telescopes situated in them but other major IR telescopes are space-based.

X-ray telescopes

High-energy X-rays are highly penetrating and are absorbed by most materials. However X-rays can be reflected by a highly polished iridium-coated mirror at shallow 'grazing' angles and brought to a focus forming an image in a detector at the focal point, as shown in Figure 7.

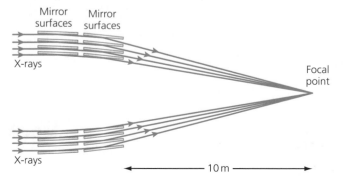

Figure 7 X-ray telescopes focus X-rays with very shallow reflections

The **aperture** of a telescope is the diameter of the hole that the electromagnetic radiation passes through before being focused onto a telescope detector.

Knowledge check 6

Explain why the Earth's atmosphere is a major limiting factor in the location of radio, IR and UV telescopes.

Summary

- A ray diagram illustrating image formation by a refracting telescope in normal adjustment is shown in Figure 1.
- The angular magnification of a refracting telescope in normal adjustment, M, is given by:

$$M = \frac{\text{angle subtended by image at eye}}{\text{angle subtended by object at unaided eye}} = \frac{f_o}{f_e}$$

  where f_o and f_e are the focal lengths of the objective and eyepiece lenses respectively.

- The Cassegrain reflecting telescope arrangement uses a parabolic concave primary mirror and a convex secondary mirror.
- A ray diagram illustrating the path of rays through a Cassegrain reflecting telescope to the eyepiece is shown in Figure 3.
- The advantages of reflecting telescopes include: easier to manufacture and support large mirrors; do not suffer from chromatic aberration; curved mirrors suffer far less from spherical aberration; very large mirrors can be made and supported easily by the telescope mount.
- The advantages of refracting telescopes include: low maintenance; optics are mechanically stable; not affected by the small secondary mirror blocking some of the light from entering the imaging system for a reflector, or the secondary mirrors and their supports in reflectors causing some diffraction of the light, blurring the image slightly.

- The collecting power of a telescope is proportional to the square of its diameter.
- Chromatic aberration is the blurring of an image because different colours of light are refracted along different paths through a lens.
- Spherical aberration is the blurring of an image due to light from different parts of the mirror or lens going to different focal points.
- The minimum angular resolution of a telescope is given by the Rayleigh criterion:

$$\theta \approx \frac{\lambda}{D}$$

- The unit of angle used for telescopes is the radian.
- The human eye and charge-coupled devices (CCDs) are the usual detectors in telescopes. Table 2 shows a comparison of these two detectors in terms of quantum efficiency and resolution.
- Radio telescopes work in a similar way to reflecting telescopes. A parabolic reflector reflects the radio waves into a detector. Because radio waves have much longer wavelengths than light waves, radio telescopes generally have much larger apertures and higher collecting powers, but much smaller resolving powers.

Classification of stars

Classification by luminosity

The **brightness** of a star that we can see in the night sky depends on the **luminosity** of the star and how far it is from Earth.

The Hipparcos scale is used to measure the brightness of stars. The Greek astronomer Hipparcos developed a six-point scale over 2000 years ago. He rated the brightest visible stars as 'first magnitude' stars and the dimmest visible stars as 'sixth magnitude' stars. Today we call the magnitude of a star as observed from Earth its **apparent magnitude**, m. The Hipparcos scale is related to the (modern) brightness of the star and a difference of 1 in apparent magnitude is equivalent to a 2.51 times change in brightness. Apparent magnitude 1 stars are therefore $2.51^5 \approx 100$ times brighter than apparent magnitude 6 stars.

The **brightness** of a star is a measure of how much visible light from the star reaches our eyes.

The **luminosity** of a star is the total energy it emits per second at all wavelengths emitted.

The **apparent magnitude**, m, of a star is a measure of its brightness as it appears in the sky.

Absolute magnitude, M

The **absolute magnitude**, M, of a star is defined as the apparent magnitude that the star would have if it were a standard distance of 10 parsecs away. Absolute magnitude is related to the luminosity of a star.

The parsec is a unit of distance defined by the concept of parallax, which is the apparent shift in the position of a star against the very distant background stars due to a change in the position of the observer, as shown in Figure 8.

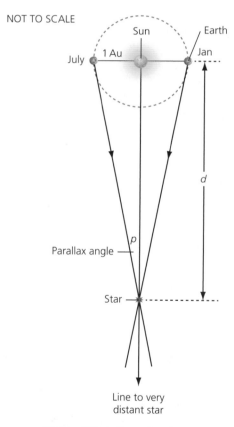

Figure 8 Parallax of a star

The **parallax** of a star as seen from Earth is due to the change in position of the Earth in its orbit around the Sun. The average distance of the Earth from the Sun is 1 **astronomical unit** (AU), equivalent to 1.5×10^{11} m. Stars with a parallax angle of 1 arcsecond due to this parallax are said to be 1 **parsec** (pc) away. 1 pc is equivalent to 3.26 **light years** (ly), where 1 light year is the distance that light travels in 1 year (1 ly = 9.46×10^{15} m).

The **absolute magnitude**, M, of a star is defined as the apparent magnitude that the star would have if it were a standard distance of 10 parsecs away.

The **parallax** of a star is its apparent change in position as seen against the background of very distant stars due to the change in position of the Earth during its annual orbit around the Sun.

1 **astronomical unit**, AU = 1.5×10^{11} m; 1 **light year**, ly = 9.46×10^{15} m; 1 **parsec**, pc = 3.08×10^{16} m.

The closest 'star' to Earth (apart from the Sun) is the red dwarf Proxima Centauri, which is 4.24 ly away from Earth. Convert this distance to **(a)** AU and **(b)** pc.

You do not need to remember the distances of each astronomical unit in metres — they are given in your Data and Formula Book.

Absolute magnitude, M, and apparent magnitude, m, are related to each other through the relationship:

$$m - M = 5 \log_{10}\left(\frac{d}{10}\right)$$

where d is the distance of a star from Earth in parsecs.

As light travels away from a star, the energy spreads out over a wider and wider area as illustrated in Figure 9.

The apparent magnitude, m, of Proxima Centauri is 5.357. Use your answer to Knowledge check 8 to work out the absolute magnitude, M, of Proxima Centauri.

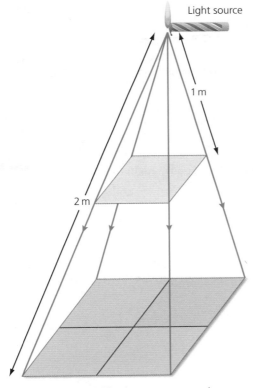

Figure 9 The inverse square law

The **inverse square law** of light intensity states that the intensity of light from a star is proportional to the inverse square of its distance away, or:

$$I = \frac{I_0}{d^2}$$

Doubling the distance from a star decreases the intensity of the light by a factor of four. This is called the **inverse square law**. It assumes that no light is absorbed by interstellar dust and gas between the source and the detector.

Classification by temperature

Stars can also be categorised by their temperature. Blue stars, such as Rigel in the constellation Orion, are very hot stars with a surface temperature of over 10 000 K. Red stars, such as the red dwarf Proxima Centauri, have much cooler surface temperatures in the order of 3000 K.

Black-body radiation

Stars can be modelled as **black-body radiators** with characteristic wavelength spectra, similar to infrared emitters here on Earth, which only depend on the absolute temperature of the object.

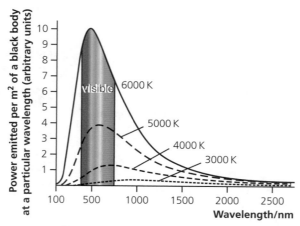

Figure 10 Black-body radiation

Black-body radiation curves have two important properties:

- The hotter the star, the higher the total amount of radiation emitted. The total power emitted is proportional to the area under the graph shown in Figure 10. Stefan's law relates the total power, P, radiated by a black-body radiator to its surface area, A, at an absolute temperature, T:

$$P = \sigma A T^4$$

where σ is the Stefan constant, equal to $5.7 \times 10^{-8}\,\text{W}\,\text{m}^{-2}\,\text{K}^{-4}$. The total power emitted by a star is called its luminosity, L.

- The peak intensity changes to a shorter wavelength as the temperature increases. Wien's displacement law states that the product of the peak wavelength, λ_{max} and the absolute temperature, T, is a constant:

$$\lambda_{max}T = \text{a constant} = 2.9 \times 10^{-3}\,\text{m}\,\text{K}$$

Knowledge check 10

The Sun has a surface temperature of 5778 K and the radius of the photosphere (the light-emitting part of the Sun) is 696 000 km. Calculate the luminosity of the Sun and the peak wavelength of its emissions.

Principles of the use of stellar spectral classes

Stars emit light with a continuous spectrum of different colours. The gases in the atmosphere of a star absorb some of these colours, forming dark absorption lines in the spectrum. The pattern of the dark absorption lines depends on both the chemical composition of the star and its temperature. Figure 11 shown an example of this.

A **black-body radiator** in thermal equilibrium (at constant temperature) emits electromagnetic radiation called black-body radiation. The black-body radiation is emitted obeying Planck's law, so that its spectrum is determined purely by its temperature and not by its shape or composition.

Exam tip

Always assume that a star behaves like a black-body radiator.

Exam tip

You do not need to know any experimental details about verifying Wien's displacement law.

Exam tip

Do not confuse luminosity and brightness. Luminosity is the total power emitted by a star at all wavelengths; brightness is a measure of only the visible light emitted by the star.

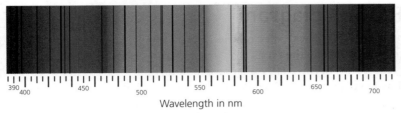

Figure 11 Absorption lines in the visible spectrum of the Sun

Astronomers discovered that the **absorption spectra** of stars could be assigned to groups, called spectral classes, with similar characteristics, as shown in Table 3.

Table 3 Stellar spectral classes

Spectral class	Intrinsic colour	Temperature/K	Prominent absorption lines
O	Blue	25000–50000	He⁺, He, H
B	Blue	11000–25000	He, H
A	Blue-white	7500–11000	H (strongest), ionised metals
F	White	6000–7500	Ionised metals
G	Yellow-white	5000–6000	Ionised and neutral metals
K	Orange	3500–5000	Neutral metals
M	Red	<3500	Neutral metals, TiO

The most common element in stars is hydrogen, and hydrogen absorption lines are observed in nearly all stellar spectra. These lines are due to electron transitions between hydrogen atom energy levels, as shown in Figure 12.

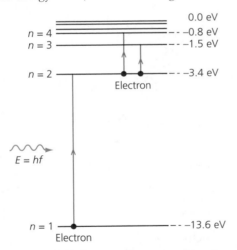

Figure 12 Hydrogen atom energy levels

At low temperatures the hydrogen electron is in its lowest (ground) state, but at higher temperatures it is raised to higher energy levels. With A- and B-class stars at temperatures between 7500 K and 25 000 K there are a significant number of atoms with electrons in the $n = 2$ energy level that are able to absorb photons, lifting them into the $n = 3, 4, 5$ etc. energy levels, and producing corresponding dark absorption lines. These lines form the Balmer absorption series.

The **absorption spectrum** of a star is the sequence of dark absorption lines in the continuous spectrum emitted by the star, corresponding to particular elements at particular temperatures.

Exam tip

In the examination you will be asked about energy level transitions to and from the $n = 2$ energy level only — these correspond to the Balmer absorption series.

Knowledge check 11

Explain how dark absorption lines are formed in the spectrum of the Sun.

The Hertzsprung–Russell diagram

The **Hertzsprung–Russell (HR) diagram** is a graph with spectral class plotted on the *x*-axis against absolute magnitude (or luminosity) on the *y*-axis. The diagram can also be plotted with temperature on the *x*-axis, in this case with a scale linking the spectral classes to their corresponding temperatures, but it could also be plotted using a logarithmic temperature scale. The positions of stars are plotted on the diagram and some general patterns appear corresponding to the main major stellar groups — main sequence stars; giant and supergiant stars; and dwarf stars, as shown in Figure 13.

The **Hertzsprung–Russell diagram** is a graph with spectral class (or temperature) plotted on the *x*-axis against absolute magnitude (or luminosity) on the *y*-axis.

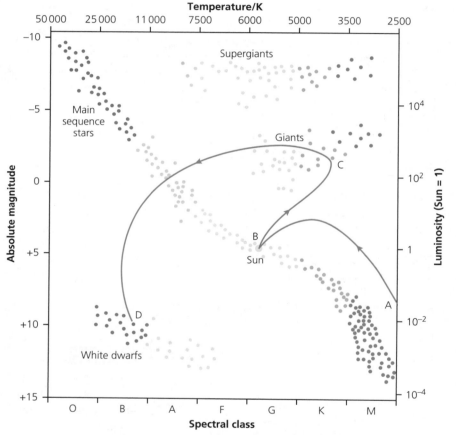

Figure 13 The Hertzsprung–Russell diagram

The HR diagram shown in Figure 13 also shows the evolutionary path taken by a Sun-like (G-class) star. The star starts as a collapsing nebula (cloud of dust and gas) forming a **protostar** at A. The protostar evolves into a **main sequence star** at B, where it spends the vast amount of its lifetime (about 10 billion years).

Towards the end of its life the star starts to run out of hydrogen and to fuse helium in large quantities. This process releases more energy (its total luminosity increases) and the star swells, forming a **red giant** at C. But as it does so its surface temperature cools as the energy released spreads out over a much larger area. The red giant phase is relatively short before the helium runs out; the star fuses progressively heavier and heavier elements but

> **Exam tip**
>
> You must be able to identify and label the position of the Sun on an HR diagram.

A **protostar** is the stage in a star's lifetime immediately before it starts to emit radiation due to nuclear fusion inside its core.

A **main sequence star** is a star in which hydrogen fusion is the dominant thermonuclear fusion mechanism. Stars tend to spend the majority of their lifetime on the main sequence.

A **red giant** is a star that is towards the end of its lifetime — it is formed when a main sequence star starts to run out of hydrogen fuel and the fusion of helium begins to dominate.

the amount of energy produced is not enough to counteract the gravitational weight of the star and it collapses in on itself. The outer atmosphere of the star is puffed off into space forming a planetary nebula and the remaining core of the star forms a **white dwarf**.

The remnant energy of the star generates a luminosity that is much smaller than the luminosity of the red giant and it moves down the HR diagram. Because this energy is mostly contained within the white dwarf, confined within a much smaller volume (and surface area), the surface temperature of the star rises and it moves towards the left of the HR diagram, joining the white dwarf group at D.

Supernovae, neutron stars and black holes

The 'death' of large, massive stars is much more violent and spectacular than the planetary nebula and white dwarf end-points of Sun-like mass and smaller stars. When the nuclear fuel is exhausted, the huge star collapses under its own weight with no radiation pressure to hold it out. The core of the star can collapse in a matter of seconds raising the temperature to over 100 billion kelvin. At these temperatures (and pressures), the protons within the core undergo electron capture forming neutrons (and a neutron star) and an immense flux of neutrinos. The core cannot collapse any further and the in-falling matter rebounds, forming an explosive shock wave called a **supernova**, as shown in Figure 14.

A **white dwarf** is the core remnant of a red giant star formed when the red giant is no longer undergoing the process of nuclear fusion.

Knowledge check 12

Compare the luminosities and surface temperatures of Sun-like main sequence stars, red giants and white dwarfs.

A **supernova** is a huge explosion at the end of the red supergiant phase of a high-mass star's lifetime. The nuclear fusion process inside the star stops and the star collapses in on itself.

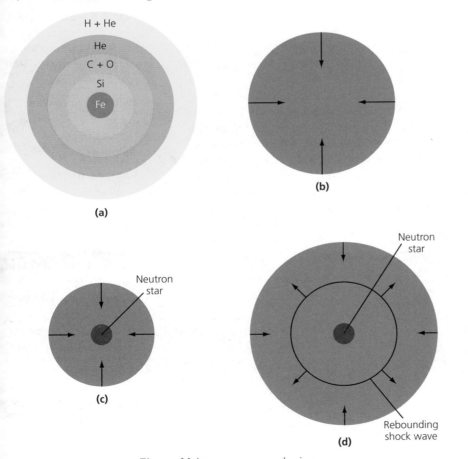

Figure 14 A supernova explosion

The nuclear fusion reactions restart in the outer atmosphere of the star because of the very high temperature of the core. This produces huge amounts of energy in a matter of seconds, and rapidly increases the absolute magnitude of the star. The shock wave then explodes, throwing this energy out into space forming a (type 2) supernova. Supernovae are some of the brightest and most energetic events in the Universe, emitting more energy in a few seconds than the Sun does in its entire lifetime. They also produce elements heavier than iron and new stars and planets are formed from the resulting nebula.

Neutron stars and black holes

Collapsing supergiant stars emit huge amounts of highly energetic gamma rays, known as gamma-ray bursts (GRBs), which last for only a few seconds as the star collapses. The neutron star that can be formed at the heart of the supernova explosion can have a mass about 1.5 times heavier than the Sun, compacted into a sphere with a radius of about 12 km. The most massive stars (more than 20 solar masses) collapse to form black holes. The resulting core is so massive that the gravitational force even collapses the resulting neutrons, and the black hole formed is so dense that not even light can escape.

The radius of a black hole beyond which the gravitational pull of the central core is so large that not even light can escape defines the *event horizon* of the black hole. This radius is called the Schwarzschild radius, R_S, and is approximated by the relationship:

$$R_S = \frac{2GM}{c^2}$$

where M is the mass of the black hole. It is thought that supermassive black holes, with a mass heavier than about 50 solar masses, form the centre of many galaxies.

Type 1a supernovae

Type 1a supernovae occur in binary star systems involving a white dwarf and commonly (but not exclusively) a red giant. Matter from the expanding red dwarf is pulled towards the white dwarf. When its mass reaches about 1.4 solar masses the white dwarf collapses, reigniting thermonuclear reactions within the white dwarf and triggering a type 1a supernova explosion. These supernovae are considered to be standard candles by astronomers because they all explode with approximately the same peak absolute magnitude. A characteristic light curve is generated as a result of the decay of nickel-56 and cobalt-56 produced during the thermonuclear reactions within the collapsing white dwarf, as shown in Figure 15. Observing these supernovae from Earth and measuring their apparent magnitude allows the distance of each supernova from Earth to be calculated.

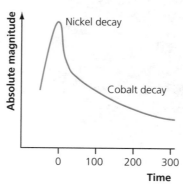

Figure 15 Type 1a supernova light curve

Knowledge check 13

Calculate the Schwarzchild radius of a star such as Betelgeuse, which has a mass of 1.5×10^{31} kg.

Knowledge check 14

Explain what is meant by a type 1a supernova.

Summary

- The apparent magnitude, m, of a star is the brightness of the star as seen from Earth.
- The Hipparcos scale is an apparent magnitude scale where the dimmest visible stars have a magnitude of 6 and the brightest visible stars have a magnitude of 1.
- The Hipparcos scale is related to the (modern) brightness of the star and a difference of 1 in apparent magnitude is equivalent to a 2.51 times change in brightness.
- The visible brightness of a star is a subjective scale of measurement.
- The absolute magnitude of a star, M, is its brightness as measured from a standard distance of 10 pc. M is related to m by $m - M = 5\log_{10}(d/10)$.
- 1 parsec (pc) is equivalent to 3.26 light years (ly), where 1 light year is the distance that light travels in 1 year (1 ly = 9.46×10^{15} m).
- Stefan's law is $P = \sigma AT^4$. It can be used to compare the power outputs, temperatures and sizes of stars.
- Wien's displacement law is $\lambda_{max}T$ = a constant $= 2.9 \times 10^{-3}$ m K. It can be used to estimate the black-body temperature of a star (assumed to be a black body) using a black-body emission curve.
- The main spectral classes of stars and some of their properties are shown in Table 3.
- The Hertzsprung–Russell (HR) diagram shows the classification of stars in the general terms of main sequence stars, dwarf stars and giant stars.

- The axis scales of a HR diagram range from –10 to +15 on the absolute magnitude axis and 50 000 K to 2500 K on the temperature axis.
- You need to be familiar with the position of the Sun on a HR diagram.
- The evolution of a star can be shown by a path on a HR diagram. Figure 13 shows the evolution path of a star similar to our Sun.
- Supernovae are explosions of red supergiant stars towards the end of their life cycle and they are characterised by rapid increases in absolute magnitude.
- Neutron stars are the collapsed cores of stars that have been part of a supernova explosion and are composed almost entirely of neutrons — they have extremely high densities.
- Black holes are the even more massive remnants of a supernova explosion. The escape velocity is faster than the speed of light for a black hole.
- Gamma-ray bursts (GRBs) are formed during the collapse of supergiant stars when they form neutron stars or black holes. GRBs emit approximately twice the total energy output of our Sun over the course of a few seconds.
- Type 1a supernovae can be used as standard candles to determine distances. The light curve for typical type 1a supernovae is shown in Figure 15.
- The event horizon for a black hole, called the Schwarzschild radius, R_S, is given by $R_S = 2GM/c^2$.

Cosmology

Cosmology is the study of the origin, behaviour and ultimate fate of the Universe. Studies are carried out by mapping the positions and movements of objects in the Universe and use the principle of the Doppler effect.

The Doppler effect and quasars

The Doppler effect involves the apparent change in wavelength (or frequency) of the light from an object in space recorded by an observer on Earth. The change is due to the relative motion of the Earth and the object. This effect is similar to the Doppler effect for sound, where the pitch of a sound increases as the object emitting the sound moves towards you, and decreases as the object moves away from you. For very distant objects, the relative motion is due to the cosmological expansion of the space between the Earth and the objects. The cosmological expansion causes most objects in the

Universe to move away from each other, increasing the wavelength of the radiation emitted by either object. For visible light this means that the radiation 'shifts' towards the red end of the spectrum, causing a *redshift*, $\Delta\lambda$. **Cosmological redshift** can be expressed as a fraction (called the z-parameter) of the original emitted wavelength, λ, or in terms of frequencies, f, where:

$$z = \frac{\Delta f}{f} = \frac{v}{c} \text{ and } \frac{\Delta\lambda}{\lambda} = -\frac{v}{c} = -z \text{ for } v \ll c$$

Exam tip

Remember, velocity is a vector quantity and, by convention, motion towards you is considered to be positive and motion away from you is considered negative. Positive Doppler shifts therefore mean objects are blue-shifting, or moving towards us, and negative Doppler shifts represent objects moving away from us, or red-shifting.

The largest observed redshifts in the Universe correspond to **quasars** (quasi-stellar radio sources) — the supercompacted region in the centre of a massive galaxy formed around a supermassive black hole. These objects were formed approximately 12 billion years ago, soon after the Big Bang, and as such are some of the most distant observable objects in the Universe. Quasars are also some of the most powerful, luminous and highest energy objects, emitting more energy than the entire Milky Way galaxy. The highest observed value of z for these objects is just over 7. These values are measured using radio-frequency radiation because quasars are extremely 'bright' radio sources.

Many stars in the Universe are in fact **binary stars**, where two stars or stellar objects orbit around a common centre of gravity. When one of the stars is moving towards the Earth relatively, the light from the star is blue-shifted (its wavelength decreases), and when it is moving away from Earth relatively, the light from the star is red-shifted (its wavelength increases), as shown in Figure 16. The relative shifts of the light from each star can be used to determine their orbital velocity.

The cosmological redshift of an object in space is its redshift due to the expansion of the Universe.

Knowledge check 15

Explain what is meant by cosmological redshift.

A quasar is a supercompacted region in the centre of a massive galaxy formed around a supermassive black hole.

Binary stars are two stellar objects orbiting around a common centre of gravity.

Knowledge check 16

Explain why quasars have some of the highest z-parameters observed.

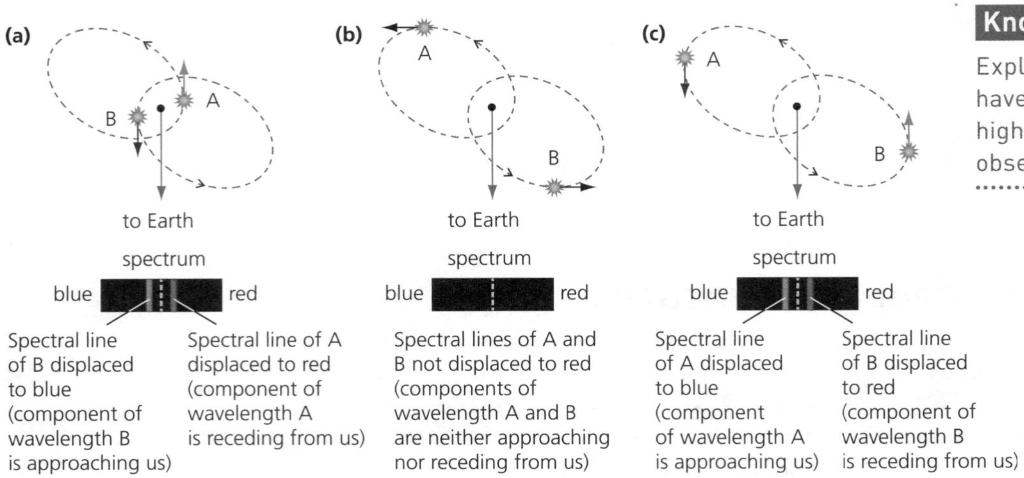

(a) to Earth
spectrum
blue   red
Spectral line of B displaced to blue (component of wavelength B is approaching us)
Spectral line of A displaced to red (component of wavelength A is receding from us)

(b) to Earth
spectrum
blue   red
Spectral lines of A and B not displaced to red (components of wavelength A and B are neither approaching nor receding from us)

(c) to Earth
spectrum
blue   red
Spectral line of A displaced to blue (component of wavelength A is approaching us)
Spectral line of B displaced to red (component of wavelength B is receding from us)

Figure 16 Binary stars and Doppler shift

Hubble's law

The relationship between the recession velocity, v, and the distance of a distant object such as a galaxy, d, is known as **Hubble's law**:

$$v = Hd$$

where H is the Hubble constant with a value of $65 \, \text{km s}^{-1} \, \text{Mpc}^{-1}$.

Knowledge check 17

A galaxy is observed to have a recessional velocity of $1320 \, \text{km s}^{-1}$. If the value of the Hubble constant is $65 \, \text{km s}^{-1} \, \text{Mpc}^{-1}$, calculate the distance of the galaxy away from Earth.

> **Hubble's law** is the relationship between the velocity of recession of a galaxy, v, and the distance of the galaxy from Earth, d, where $v = Hd$ and H is the Hubble constant.

Hubble's law was first proposed by Georges Lemaitre in 1927, but became known as Hubble's law following the astronomer Edwin Hubble's observational data on distant objects in 1929. Hubble measured the redshifts of distant objects known as 'nebulae', which were in fact other galaxies, and then converted them to velocities. Modern techniques involve the measurement of the brightness of a type 1a supernova (from which the distance can be calculated) and measurement of the redshift of the light from the supernova (from which the velocity of recession can be calculated).

Today Hubble's law is interpreted using the **Big Bang theory** of the formation of the Universe. The objects observed by Hubble (and modern astronomers) are all moving away from each other because the Universe is expanding and the objects are moving with the expansion — in effect the 'space' is getting bigger between the objects. The logical conclusion from Hubble's law is that if you run the Universe backwards through time, about 13.8 billion years ago it contracts to a point called a singularity — the Universe came into being as the result of an explosion called the Big Bang.

In the first few minutes after the Big Bang, the temperature of the early Universe was hot enough for the nuclear fusion of hydrogen into helium gas, in the same way that stellar nuclear fusion takes place today within stars such as our Sun. The theories of stellar nuclear fusion predict the ratio of hydrogen to helium in stars to be about 75% : 25% (and this is confirmed by direct observation) and this ratio is the same as the ratio observed in the most distant objects in the modern Universe (quasars), formed soon after the Big Bang itself.

Further evidence for the Big Bang theory comes from observation of the **cosmological microwave background radiation** (CMBR), which appears to come from all around us. This background radiation has a peak wavelength of 1.8 mm, corresponding to a black-body object with a temperature of about 2.7 K, which is consistent with the redshift of the radiation formed at the time of the Big Bang.

We can also use Hubble's law to determine the age of the Universe. The speed of an object can be determined using the simple equation $v = d/t$, where d is the distance of the object away from us and t is the time taken to get there. Substituting for v in Hubble's law leads to:

$$t = \frac{1}{H}$$

> The **Big Bang theory** stipulates that the Universe came into existence as the result of a huge explosion called a singularity.

> The **cosmological microwave background radiation** (CMBR), is the background radiation of the Universe with a peak wavelength of 1.8 mm, corresponding to a black-body object with a temperature of about 2.7 K and consistent with the redshift of the radiation formed at the time of the Big Bang.

Knowledge check 18

List three pieces of observational evidence for the Big Bang.

Knowledge check 19

Calculate the Hubble constant (in units of y^{-1}) if the Universe is 13.8 billion years old.

Detection of exoplanets

Exoplanets are planets that orbit stars outside our Solar System. It is difficult to observe exoplanets directly because they do not emit their own light. They are usually detected either by the Doppler shift of the star that they orbit, or by variations in the brightness of the star as the exoplanet transits across its surface as observed from Earth. Figure 17 shows how the Doppler shift method works.

An **exoplanet** is a plane orbiting a star outside our Solar System.

NOT TO SCALE

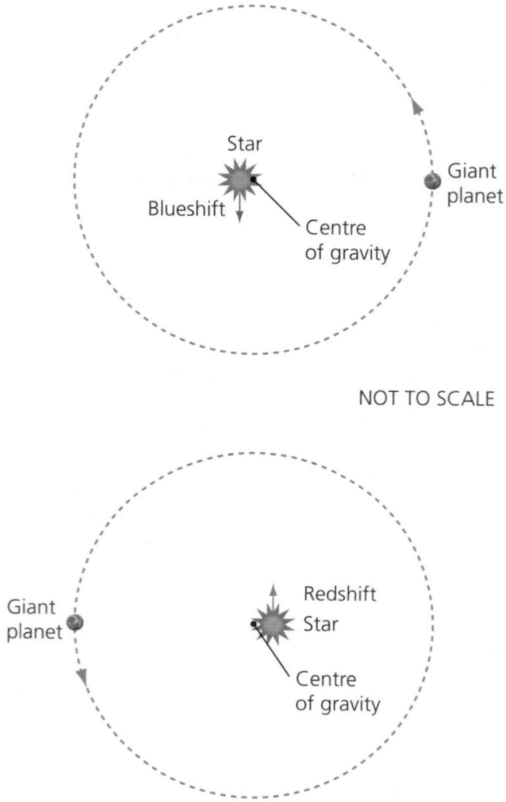

Figure 17 The Doppler shift method of exoplanet detection

A large gas giant planet and a star will orbit around a common centre of gravity, close to the star. The star will spend part of its time moving towards the Earth relatively, and part of its time moving away from the Earth relatively. Relative motion towards the Earth will result in a small blueshift of its emitted radiation and relative motion away from the Earth will result in a small redshift. Observation of these Doppler shifts indicates the presence of the large exoplanet.

Knowledge check 20

Explain why a spectral line from a star orbiting around a common centre of gravity with a large exoplanet will be 'broadened'.

The **planetary transit** method involves measuring the change in the brightness of the star as the planet moves between the star and a telescope detector on Earth. Figure 18 shows a typical light curve for a planetary transit.

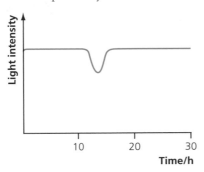

Figure 18 A typical planetary transit light curve used to observe an exoplanet

As the planet moves in front of the star, the intensity of the light observed by the telescope detector decreases. The bigger the radius of the planet, the larger the drop in intensity.

Summary

- The cosmological redshift is given by the z-parameter:
$$z = \frac{\Delta f}{f} = \frac{v}{c} \text{ and } \frac{\Delta \lambda}{\lambda} = -\frac{v}{c} = -z \text{ for } v \ll c$$
- Binary stars produce a Doppler shift in the wavelengths of light emitted due to apparent motion towards and away from Earth as the two stars orbit a common centre of gravity.
- Quasars are the most distant measurable objects and are bright radio sources. They show large optical redshifts and huge power outputs.
- Galaxies and quasars (supercompacted regions in the centre of a massive galaxy formed around a supermassive black hole) produce large redshifts because they are very far away and moving very fast.
- Hubble's law relates the velocity of recession of an object v, to its distance, d, away from Earth — it states that $v = Hd$, where H is the Hubble constant.

- The Universe shows a cosmological redshift due its expansion, with all but the very closest stars undergoing a redshift.
- The age of the Universe, t, can be estimated using the Hubble constant using $t = 1/H$.
- The Universe came into being approximately 13.8 billion years ago as the result of a huge explosion called the Big Bang. Evidence for this event comes from cosmological microwave background radiation (CMBR), and the relative abundances of hydrogen and helium.
- It is difficult to detect exoplanets directly. Most exoplanets are detected indirectly using the variation in the Doppler shift (radial velocity method) of their parent star, or they are detected by changes in the intensity of their parent star's light output as measured from Earth using its light curve, as shown in Figure 18.

■ Turning points in physics

The discovery of the electron

Cathode rays

In 1838, Michael Faraday performed a series of experiments attempting to pass an electric current through a glass tube with some of the air pumped out, as shown in Figure 19.

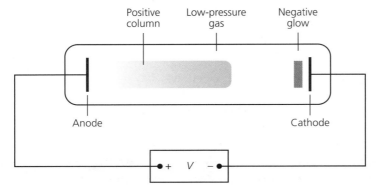

Figure 19 Michael Faraday's glass discharge tube

He noticed a faint glow starting at the cathode and, as more air was pumped out of the tube, the faint glow appeared to travel further along the tube towards the anode. These 'rays' became known as **cathode rays**.

In 1897, J. J. Thomson carried out several important experiments on these cathode rays, using improved glassware and better vacuum pumps, and he discovered that they were deflected by both electric fields and magnetic fields. He also measured their specific charge (charge per unit mass). Thomson concluded that these rays were streams of tiny, negatively charged particles that he called 'corpuscles' — they were later renamed 'electrons'.

Thermionic emission of electrons

Cathode rays (beams of electrons) are produced in a process called **thermionic emission**. As electric current is passed through a metal wire filament, the wire heats up, conducting electrons near the surface gain more kinetic energy and eventually they can escape from the surface of the wire. Inside a vacuum tube, there are no air particles to interact with the emitted electrons and they can be repelled from the metal filament (if it is the cathode) and attracted towards a distant anode. The higher the potential difference, V, between the two electrodes, the higher the kinetic energy acquired by the accelerating electrons. The work done on the electrons is equal to their gain in kinetic energy so:

$$\frac{1}{2}mv^2 = eV$$

where m is the mass of an electron, e is the charge on the electron and v is the maximum velocity of the electron as it hits the anode.

Cathode rays are beams of electrons emitted from a metal cathode electrode when an electric current passes through a vacuum.

Thermionic emission is the emission of electrons from a hot metal filament cathode.

Exam tip

You should assume that the velocity of electrons in questions involving cathode rays are too small for relativity to be taken into account, unless otherwise stated.

Knowledge check 21

Calculate the velocity of an electron accelerated through a potential difference of 4500 V inside a cathode ray tube. Assume non-relativistic velocities.

Specific charge of the electron

The specific charge on an electron, e/m, can be determined using modern school laboratory equipment using a method similar to Thomson's method. The apparatus is shown in Figure 20 and a schematic diagram showing the forces acting on the electron beam is shown in Figure 21.

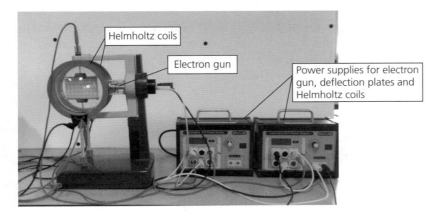

Figure 20 The equipment needed to measure the specific charge on an electron in the school laboratory

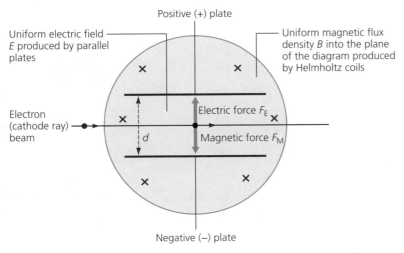

Figure 21 Schematic diagram showing the forces acting on an electron beam inside an electron deflection tube

Content Guidance

A beam of electrons is produced by an electron gun using an EHT supply with a voltage between 3000 and 5000 V. The electron beam enters the tube and is subject to a vertical force due to an **electric field** produced by a potential difference of about 12 V DC between the two horizontal metal plates. This force causes the electron beam to move upwards in a parabolic arc. The size of the force on the electrons is given by:

$$F_E = eE = \frac{eV}{d}$$

where E is the strength of the electric field (in newtons per coulomb, $N\,C^{-1}$), e is the charge on the electron (in coulombs, C), V is the potential difference across the two parallel plates (in volts, V) and d is the separation of the plates (in metres, m).

A **magnetic field** is then applied to the tube using a current passing through the two Helmholtz coils. The magnetic field is arranged so that it exerts a force at right angles to the direction of travel of the beam and vertically downwards inside the two parallel plates, in the opposite direction to the force due to the electric field. The magnitude of the magnetic force is given by:

$$F_M = Bev$$

where B is the magnetic field strength (in tesla, T), e is the charge on the electron (in coulombs, C) and v is the velocity of the electrons (in metres per second, $m\,s^{-1}$).

The current through the coils and the voltage across the plates are then adjusted so that the two forces balance and the electron beam travels in a straight line through the tube. In this case:

$$F_E = F_M \Rightarrow \frac{eV}{d} = Bev \Rightarrow \frac{V}{d} = Bv \Rightarrow v = \frac{V}{Bd} \qquad \text{Equation 1}$$

The electric field inside the tube is then switched off and the current in the coils adjusted again to make the electron beam move in a circle, where:

$$Bev = \frac{mv^2}{r} \Rightarrow v = \frac{Ber}{m} \qquad \text{Equation 2}$$

Equating Equation 1 and Equation 2 and rearranging:

$$\frac{Ber}{m} = \frac{V}{Bd} \Rightarrow \frac{e}{m} = \frac{V}{B^2rd}$$

All the values of V, B, r and d are easily measured allowing the specific charge of the electron to be calculated.

As a result of his experiments in 1897, Thomson reached several conclusions:

- Electrons are negatively charged — because of the direction of deflection of the particles in the tube.
- Cathode rays were not a new form of electromagnetic wave (as had been suggested by Helmholtz) — because the charge could not be separated from the particles.
- The charge-to-mass ratio for all the particles is the same — when Thomson changed the gas in the discharge tube it did not alter the value, so the specific charge was a fundamental property of the particles and not the measuring equipment.

The **electric field** between two horizontal metal plates is the force per unit charge experienced by an electric charge situated between the plates, $E = F_E/Q$.

A **magnetic field** is a place where a magnetic monopole experiences a force.

Exam tip

The velocity of electrons in an electron diffraction tube is generally much lower than the speed of light and relativistic effects can be ignored.

Exam tip

Do not be confused between the velocity of an electron, v, and the accelerating voltage, V.

Knowledge check 22

Calculate the specific charge on an electron from an electron deflection tube experiment in which $V = 11.5\,V$; $r = 22\,mm$; $d = 25\,mm$ and $B = 0.35\,mT$.

Thomson calculated the e/m value for the electron to be more than 1800 times higher than that of the smallest known ion, hydrogen. The specific charge of the electron is $1.76 \times 10^{11}\,\mathrm{C\,kg^{-1}}$ whereas the specific charge of a hydrogen ion (or proton) is $9.6 \times 10^{7}\,\mathrm{C\,kg^{-1}}$.

Thomson's experiments provided the first direct evidence for subatomic particles.

Knowledge check 23

Explain why Thomson was unable to measure the actual charge on the electron.

Millikan's determination of the electronic charge, e

Soon after Thomson determined a value for e/m, other physicists started to perform experiments to measure the value of the charge on the electron independently of its mass. In 1913, the American physicist Robert Millikan published a paper detailing his work on measuring the charge on the electron using charged oil drops falling between two electrode plates. Millikan measured the value of e to be $(1.592 \pm 0.003) \times 10^{-19}\,\mathrm{C}$, which, although slightly lower than the accepted value of $1.602 \times 10^{-19}\,\mathrm{C}$, was a remarkable achievement in 1913 — Millikan was later awarded a Nobel prize in 1923 for this work.

A diagram illustrating Millikan's experimental apparatus is shown in Figure 22.

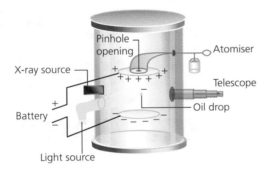

Figure 22 A schematic diagram of Millikan's apparatus used to measure the fundamental charge on the electron, e

A small charged drop of fine oil spray is held stationary between two oppositely charged plates (with the positive plate above the negative plate). The condition for holding a charged oil droplet, of charge Q, stationary between oppositely charged parallel plates is given by:

$$\frac{QV}{d} = mg$$

where mg is the weight of the oil droplet acting downwards, and QV/d is the upward force on the oil drop due to the electric field (Q is the overall charge on the drop; V is the potential difference between the two plates and d is the separation of the plates). Millikan assumed that the charge on the oil drop must have an integer value (or quantisation), n, of the charge on the electron, e, so:

$$\frac{neV}{d} = mg$$

Knowledge check 24

In Millikan's apparatus, one particular oil drop had a mass of $1.3 \times 10^{-15}\,\mathrm{kg}$. The PD across the plates in his experiment was 1000 V and the plates were separated by a distance of 25 mm. Calculate the charge, Q, on the drop and suggest a value for n.

Content Guidance

Millikan then used **Stokes' law** to determine a value for the weight of an oil drop. Stokes' law allows the determination of the viscous force on an oil droplet falling at terminal velocity, v, through a fluid such as air. At terminal velocity, this force will be equal to the weight of the drop:

$$F = 6\pi\eta rv$$

where η is the viscosity of the fluid and r is the radius of the drop. The weight of the oil drop, mg, can be equated with this force at terminal velocity, with the mass term replaced using the density of the oil:

$$6\pi\eta rv = mg = \frac{4}{3}\pi r^3 \rho g$$

Rearranging this equation to give r, the radius of the drop:

$$r = \sqrt{\frac{9\eta v}{2\rho g}}$$

The radius can then be used to calculate the mass of the drop, m, and substituted back into:

$$\frac{neV}{d} = mg$$

All the values in this equation are known with the exception of n and e. Millikan then used X-rays to ionise the oil drops that he sprayed into the chamber using an atomiser. The oil drops acquired different integer charges and by selecting different drops to measure (Millikan actually based his calculations on 58 drops), he was able to determine a value for e — and in the process proved that charge is quantised.

> **Stokes' law** is the relationship between the viscous force, F, on an object moving through a fluid such as air at a terminal velocity, v, given by $F = 6\pi\eta rv$, where η is the viscosity of the fluid.

> **Exam tip**
>
> Assume that the effect of buoyancy on the drop are negligible.

> **Knowledge check 25**
>
> Explain why Millikan based his calculations of the value of e on 58 different drops.

Summary

- 'Cathode rays' was the name initially given to the beams of electrons emitted when an electric current travels between the cathode and anode of a vacuum discharge tube.
- Electrons are emitted by hot cathode metal wire filaments by the process of thermionic emission.
- The work done on an electron accelerated through a PD of V is equal to its kinetic energy gained and is given by $\frac{1}{2}mv^2 = eV$.
- The specific charge, e/m, of an electron can be measured in a school laboratory using an electron deflection tube and an electric field combined with the magnetic field produced by two Helmholtz coils surrounding the tube.
- The specific charge of the electron was first measured by Thomson in 1897 and he concluded that: electrons are negatively charged; cathode rays were not electromagnetic waves; the specific charge was the same for all electrons and is a fundamental property of the particles.

- Millikan measured the charge on the electron in 1913 by observing charged oil droplets, of charge Q, held stationary between two oppositely charged parallel plates, where $QV/d = mg$.
- The motion of a falling oil droplet with and without an electric field can be used to measure the terminal velocity of the drop and hence its mass, which is then used to calculate its charge.
- Stokes' law for the viscous force on an oil droplet is used to calculate the droplet radius, which is needed to determine the mass of the droplet. Stokes' law is written as $F = 6\pi\eta rv$.
- Millikan managed to measure the charge on an electron independent of its mass for the first time, and realised that electric charge is quantised.

Wave–particle duality

Newton's corpuscular theory of light

Isaac Newton published his corpuscular theory of light in 1690 — he proposed that light propagates away from a source as a series of tiny particles or **corpuscles**. This theory rivalled the wave theory of light published by Christiaan Huygens in 1678. Newton's corpuscular theory was able to explain the reflection, refraction and dispersion of light and, as a consequence of the emission of the 'corpuscles', the source should lose mass. Huygens' theory proposed that light propagates as a longitudinal wave (like sound), and because longitudinal waves need a medium to propagate through, Huygens also proposed that 'space' was filled with a substance called the **æther**, which was transparent and had no inertia (or mass).

In this theory, waves moved through different materials by the propagation of wavefronts and each point on the original wavefront acts as a new point source of (secondary) wavelets, which then spread out. The secondary wavelets then combine to form a new wavefront, as shown in Figure 23.

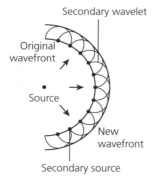

Figure 23 Huygens' construction showing the propagation of wavefronts

Huygens theory could also explain the reflection, refraction and dispersion of light. Both Newton's and Huygens' theories had their merits and weaknesses. They could both explain most of the properties of light understood in the late 1600s, but neither could be 'proved' at the time because there was no way of measuring the speed of light — and because the existence of the æther could not be proved, Newton's theory was accepted and held sway for 150 years.

Significance of Young's double slit experiment

In 1804, the English physicist Thomas Young published the results of a series of experiments he had performed. He had observed the 'shadows' produced by a very narrow beam of sunlight as it passed through small holes, slits or fine-edged objects. Young observed a series of 'fringes', particularly when he passed the beam through a pair of very close, fine slits in an arrangement now known as the Young's double slit experiment. Young observed that the spacing of the fringes depended on: the separation of the slits; the wavelength (colour) of the light; and the distance of the slit from the screen that was used to image the fringes. A modern version of Young's experimental set-up is shown in Figure 24.

Corpuscles was the name given by Newton to particles of light — we now call them photons.

The **æther** was the name proposed by Huygens for the 'medium' that light moves through when propagating through space.

Knowledge check 26

State the difference between Newton's theory of light and Huygens' theory of light.

Knowledge check 27

Which of the following effects cannot be explained using Newton's theory of light: reflection and/ or refraction and/or diffraction?

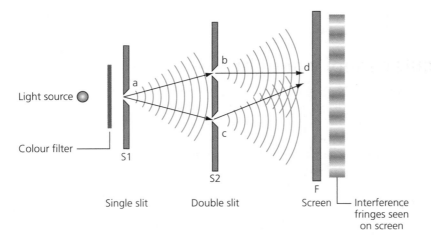

Figure 24 Young's double slit experiment

Young's observations could not be explained using Newton's corpuscular theory and Huygens' wave theory once again came into acceptance.

Electromagnetic waves

In 1864, James Clerk Maxwell published a paper detailing his theories about the connection between electricity and magnetism. Part of these predicted the existence of 'electromagnetic radiation', which he deduced moved with a speed c in a vacuum. Maxwell suggested that c was linked to the magnetic and electrical properties of the vacuum by the equation:

$$c = \frac{1}{\sqrt{\mu_0 \varepsilon_0}}$$

where μ_0 is the **permeability of free space** (which relates to the magnetic flux density due to a current-carrying wire in free space) and ε_0 is the **permittivity of free space** (which relates to the electric field strength due to a charged object in free space).

Maxwell suggested that electromagnetic radiation propagates as a wave of oscillating electric and magnetic fields at right angles to each other, as shown in Figure 25.

The **permeability of free space**, μ_0, relates to the magnetic flux density due to a current-carrying wire in free space.

The **permittivity of free space**, ε_0, relates to the electric field strength due to a charged object in free space.

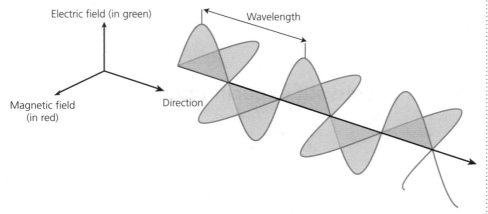

Figure 25 An electromagnetic wave showing the electric and magnetic fields at right angles to each other

All parts of the electromagnetic spectrum propagate like this, and also travel at the same speed in a vacuum — the differences are in the wavelengths and amplitudes of the different parts.

The value of the speed of light proposed by Maxwell's equation was in close agreement with a measurement made by Hippolyte Fizeau from an experiment that he carried out in 1849. In his experiment, Fizeau passed a beam of light through a 720 fine-toothed wheel rotating at 12.6 revolutions per second. The beam was therefore split into a series of very fast flashes that travelled from one hill outside Paris to another hill 8.6 km away, and then reflected back from a parabolic mirror to an eyepiece next to the light source. The flashes directly from the source and those from the distant hill were combined within the eyepiece producing a series of maximum intensity flashes and minimum intensity flashes as the speed of the toothed wheel was altered slightly. Fizeau used his measurements to calculate the speed of light to be 313 274 000 m s^{-1}. Maxwell's value was 310 740 000 m s^{-1} — a difference of less than 1%, and related to a vacuum not air. Fizeau also used a variant of this experiment to pass the beam of light through water rather than air and determined that the speed of light in water is different from that in air, as predicted by Huygens' wave theory.

Maxwell's equations also predicted the existence of other forms of electromagnetic radiation, unknown at the time of the publication of his ideas when only light, ultraviolet and infrared had been identified. In 1887, Heinrich Hertz discovered radio waves, Wilhelm Roentgen discovered X-rays in 1895 and Paul Villard discovered gamma rays in 1900.

Hertz discovered radio waves experimentally by generating a spark (fast-moving charges) between two spherical electrodes which was detected using an 'aerial' made from an incomplete loop of copper wire terminated with two more small metal spheres. Sparking in the first circuit caused the aerial loop to spark. Hertz noted that the radio waves generated by the first spark were absorbed by a metal plate, but propagated through non-metals. He was also able to focus the radio waves back onto the aerial by using a metal parabolic reflector, increasing the intensity of the sparks.

Using a flat metal sheet reflector, Hertz was able to set up a series of radio standing waves between the reflector and the source. Using his aerial, he measured the distance between adjacent positions of maximum intensity and determined the wavelength of the radio waves. Using the frequency of the radio wave generating apparatus, he calculated the speed of the radio waves to be similar to the value predicted by Maxwell.

The discovery of photoelectricity

All objects with a temperature above absolute zero emit radiation, mostly in the form of infrared radiation. The frequency and wavelength of the radiation emitted depend on the temperature of the object and the nature of its surface. A very hot object emits visible light and as the temperature of the object increases, some ultraviolet (UV) radiation is emitted, but the intensity of the emitted UV radiation drops quickly to zero. This is shown by the spectrum of a black-body emitter in Figure 26.

Classical wave theory predicted that the energy emitted by a black body would continue to increase as the wavelength decreased. This is not shown by the observations and is known as the **ultraviolet catastrophe**.

> **Knowledge check 30**
>
> Explain why Fizeau's measurement of the speed of light was important to Maxwell.

> **Knowledge check 31**
>
> Explain how Hertz measured the wavelength of his radio waves.

> The **ultraviolet catastrophe** is the lack of emission of UV radiation at high temperatures, as predicted by classical wave theory.

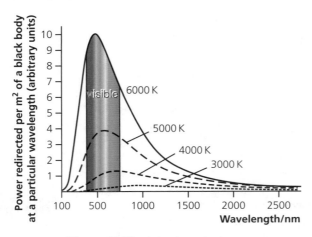

Figure 26 Black-body emission

In 1900, Max Planck proposed a theory to explain the electromagnetic emissions from a black body based on experimental observations. To do this he assumed that electromagnetic radiation was emitted in very small 'packets' called quanta or **photons**, where the energy of each quantum is given by:

$$E = nhf$$

where n is an integer (1, 2, 3…), h is a constant now known as the Planck constant and f is the frequency of the atomic oscillators in the black body emitting the radiation. Planck's theory matched the experimental observations perfectly (unlike classical wave theory).

In 1887, as part of his research into radio waves, Hertz discovered that UV radiation, shone onto the electrodes of his radio apparatus, increased the length of the sparks produced. Other physicists investigated this effect, known as the **photoelectric effect**, and in 1905 Albert Einstein published a paper explaining the observations using Planck's concept of quantised electromagnetic radiation, where the energy of each photon, E, is given by $E = hf$:

1　The incident photons have a threshold frequency below which no photoelectrons are emitted. Photoelectrons can leave the surface of the metal if they interact with a single incident photon. If the incident photon does not have enough energy (the frequency is too small), the electrons are not given enough energy to leave.

2　The energy required to leave the surface of the metal depends on the type of metal. The minimum energy required to emit photoelectrons is called the work function, ϕ, of the metal.

3　Increasing the intensity of the incident radiation increases the number of photoelectrons emitted, but it does not increase their maximum kinetic energy because the energy of the incident photons depends on their frequency, not their intensity.

4　The maximum kinetic energy of the emitted photoelectrons is dictated by the energy (and therefore frequency) of the incident photons, provided that it is greater than the work function of the metal surface.

Knowledge check 32

What is the ultraviolet catastrophe?

A **photon** is a quantum of electromagnetic radiation.

The **photoelectric effect** is the emission of photoelectrons by a metal surface when photons (of mostly UV radiation) are incident on the metal surface with energy greater than the work function of the metal surface.

Knowledge check 33

What is the photoelectric effect?

Einstein stated that:

$$hf = E_{kmax} + \phi$$

where hf is the energy of the incident photons (of frequency f); E_{kmax} is the maximum kinetic energy of the emitted photoelectrons and ϕ is the work function of the metal surface.

Knowledge check 34

Calculate the kinetic energy of photoelectrons emitted from a potassium surface with a work function of 2.3 eV, if the surface is irradiated with UV photons with energy of 2.7 eV.

Exam tip

The energies involved in the photoelectric effect are very small and can be given in terms of either joules, J, or electronvolts, eV. Remember that $1\,eV = 1.6 \times 10^{-19}\,J$.

Wave–particle duality

In 1924, Louis de Broglie proposed that particles have **wave–particle duality**. Depending on the scale of the experiment, and the detection systems involved, they will behave like waves (undergoing reflection, refraction and diffraction, for example) or behave like particles (for example, in the photoelectric effect). de Broglie proposed that the wavelength, λ, of these 'wavicles' was related to their momentum, p, by the equation:

$$p = h/\lambda$$

where h is the Planck constant.

A series of low-energy **electron diffraction** experiments by Clinton Davisson and Lester Germer in the late 1920s confirmed de Broglie's hypothesis. A diagram of a modern school laboratory electron diffraction experiment is shown in Figure 27.

Wave–particle duality is the term used to describe the behaviour of (mostly) quantum scale objects having wave-like and particle-like properties, depending on the nature of the experiment used to observe them.

Electron diffraction occurs due to the wave–particle duality of electrons. A beam of electrons passing through a graphite grid will undergo diffraction, producing a characteristic pattern on a screen.

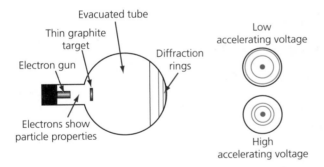

Figure 27 An electron diffraction tube with the patterns obtained by altering the accelerating voltage between the anode and cathode in the electron gun

If the accelerating voltage is V, then the wavelength, λ, of the electrons in an electron diffraction tube is given by:

$$\lambda = \frac{h}{\sqrt{2meV}}$$

where m is the (non-relativistic) mass of the electron, and e is the charge on the electron. You can see from the equation that $\lambda \propto 1/\sqrt{V}$ so increasing V reduces λ. This in turn reduces the radius of the electron diffraction pattern.

Knowledge check 35

Calculate the wavelength of electrons with a mass of $9.11 \times 10^{-31}\,kg$ travelling at a velocity of $1.2 \times 10^8\,m\,s^{-1}$.

Electron microscopes

Following de Broglie's hypothesis and the work of Davisson and Germer, physicists then started to use the wave properties of electrons to develop **electron microscopes** and in 1933 Ernst Ruska produced the first working electron microscope. Electron microscopes have a distinct advantage over light microscopes because the wavelength of the electron 'wavicles' is much lower than the wavelength of visible light and, as such, increases the resolving power of the microscope allowing much smaller objects to be imaged. The accelerating voltage, V, of the electrons required to produce a wavelength, λ, and hence image objects with a size similar to λ, can be determined by:

$$\lambda = \frac{h}{\sqrt{2meV}} \Rightarrow V = \frac{h^2}{2me\lambda^2}$$

There are two main types of electron microscope — transmission electron microscopes (TEM) and scanning tunnelling microscopes (STM).

In a TEM, a beam of electrons is produced by an electron gun and the beam is focused onto a thin target sample using magnets. The electron waves are scattered by the sample and then refocused by two further magnetic 'lenses', and a magnified image forms on a fluorescent screen or an electronic detector. The basic principle of a TEM is shown in Figure 28.

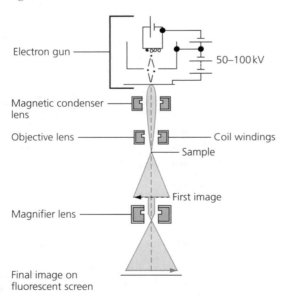

Figure 28 A transmission electron microscope

STMs work in a slightly different way. They use a very fine-tipped needle probe, which moves across, or scans, a small surface area of a specimen, as shown in Figure 29.

An **electron microscope** is a device for imaging microscopic objects at resolutions greater than a light microscope by using the wave–particle duality of a beam of electrons.

Knowledge check 3

State how electrons are focused in a TEM.

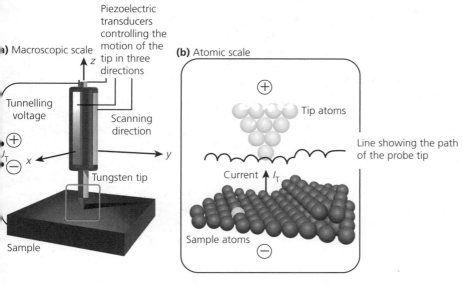

Figure 29 A scanning tunnelling electron microscope

The slightly positively charged needle probe tip is held very close to the surface of the specimen (typically no more than 1 nm above the surface) by a series of **piezoelectric transducers**. At this short distance, electrons can 'tunnel' across the gap causing a tunnelling current to flow. The tunnelling current changes as the tip moves up and down relative to the surface, increasing as it gets closer to the surface and decreasing as it moves further away.

STMs are used in two different ways:

Constant current mode — the tunnelling current is kept constant and the needle-tip is moved up and down relative to the surface. The distance moved by the tip is mapped by the machine.

Constant height mode — the distance between the needle tip and the surface is kept constant and the machine maps the tunnelling current that is related to the distance of the tip to the surface.

A **piezoelectric transducer** is a small crystal of a material that changes its shape when a potential difference is applied across it. The amount of deformation of the crystal depends on the size of the potential difference across it.

Knowledge check 37

How is the surface of a sample mapped by a STM in constant current mode?

Summary

■ Newton's corpuscular theory of light considered light to behave as a stream of particles, contrary to Huygens' wave theory. Both theories can explain reflection and refraction, but Huygens' theory required light to move through a medium that he called the æther, which could not be observed, so Newton's theory was preferred at the time.

■ Young's double slit experiment is illustrated in Figure 24. The fringes observed during this experiment showed that the light was undergoing diffraction and interference and so behaving as a wave.

■ Huygens' wave theory of light was accepted as an explanation of the nature of light as a result of Young's double slit experiment.

■ Electromagnetic radiation propagates as a wave of oscillating electric fields and magnetic fields at right angles to each other, as shown in Figure 25.

→

- Maxwell deduced a formula for the speed, c, of electromagnetic waves in a vacuum, given by:

$$c = 1 \big/ \sqrt{\mu_0 \varepsilon_0}$$

where μ_0 is the permeability of free space (which relates to the magnetic flux density due to a current-carrying wire in free space) and ε_0 is the permittivity of free space (which relates to the electric field strength due to a charged object in free space).

- Fizeau measured the speed of light in 1849 using a beam of light that passed through a fine-toothed rotating wheel. The pulses produced reflected back from a distant mirror and set up interference patterns with light that came directly from the source. Fizeau's value for c was in very close agreement with Maxwell's value.

- Hertz discovered radio waves in 1887 by generating a spark between two electrodes. The spark was detected using an 'aerial' made from an incomplete loop of copper wire. Hertz measured the speed of radio waves by using the standing waves produced when the radio waves reflected from a metal plate.

- All objects with a temperature above absolute zero emit radiation, with an emission pattern that depends on temperature and resembles a black-body radiator.

- Classical wave theory suggests that black-body radiators should continue to emit large amounts of UV radiation as they get hotter and hotter. This does not happen and is called the ultraviolet catastrophe.

- Planck interpreted the UV catastrophe and the patterns of emission by a black-body radiator by suggesting that light was quantised into photons of energy, $E = hf$.

- Classical wave theory cannot explain the observations from photoelectric effect experiments.

- Einstein used Planck's photon theory to explain the photoelectric effect. His photoelectric effect equation is $hf = E_{kmax} + \phi$, where hf is the energy of the incident photon, E_{kmax} is the maximum kinetic energy of the emitted photoelectrons and ϕ is the work function of the metal surface.

- de Broglie suggested that matter particles can behave as a wave, with a wavelength, λ, given by the equation $p = h/\lambda$, where p is the momentum of the particle.

- In an electron diffraction tube, electrons are made to diffract through a thin sample of graphite, producing a characteristic ringed diffraction pattern. The wavelength of the electrons in the beam is given by: $\lambda = h \big/ \sqrt{2meV}$ where V is the accelerating potential difference.

- Increasing the accelerating potential difference in an electron diffraction tube increases the velocity of the electrons, decreasing their wavelength. This causes the ringed diffraction pattern to contract.

- Electron microscopes have a much higher resolving power than light microscopes because the wavelength of the electrons is significantly smaller than that of light.

- The accelerating voltage, V, required to produce electron wavelengths of size λ is given by:

$$V = h^2 / 2me\lambda^2$$

- The principle of operation of a transmission electron microscope (TEM) is shown in Figure 28.

- The principle of operation of a scanning tunnelling microscope (STM) is shown in Figure 29.

Special relativity

The Michelson–Morley experiment

In Huygens' classical wave theory, light requires a medium to propagate through — Huygens called this the 'luminiferous æther' (or just the æther). The speed of light could then be explained in terms of its **absolute motion** relative to the 'static' æther. In 1897, Albert Michelson and Edward Morley published the results of their

Absolute motion is the movement of an object compared to a fixed frame of reference.

experiments to measure some of the 'properties' of the æther and, in one of the most famous **null experiments** of all time, concluded that the æther did not exist.

Michelson and Morley's experiment involved the development of an interferometer as shown in Figure 30.

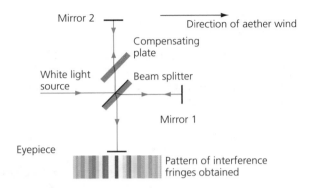

Figure 30 The Michelson–Morley interferometer

White light from a source is sent two ways through the apparatus, and it is then recombined to produce an interference pattern. In one direction (towards and back from mirror 1) the beam of light moves with and against the æther; in the other direction (towards and back from mirror 2) it moves perpendicular to the æther. If the æther exists, there should be a difference in the speed of light in both directions. The beam of light should take slightly longer to travel to and from mirror 1 (parallel to the direction of motion of the Earth through the æther) than the beam travelling to and from mirror 2 (perpendicular to the motion of the Earth through the æther) and the interference pattern should change as the whole apparatus is rotated horizontally so that mirrors 1 and 2 change positions.

Michelson and Morley observed no noticeable changes in the interference pattern as the apparatus was rotated through 90°. It was concluded that the æther did not exist and that the speed of light was invariant (constant) — in other words, it was the same in all directions irrespective of the motion of the object emitting it.

Einstein's theory of special relativity

The Michelson–Morley experiment's destruction of the æther theory requires all motion in the Universe to be 'relative'. There can be no 'origin', or fixed reference frame that motion can be compared to and this required a new theory for the motion of objects moving through space, particularly at high speeds faster than about 50% of the speed of light. In 1905, Einstein published his first great paper on relativity detailing the theory of **special relativity**, in which objects move relative to each other at constant velocities. His theory of general relativity concerning accelerating objects was published in 1915.

Einstein's theory of special relativity introduced the concept of **inertial frames of reference** in which two observers are moving relative to one another at constant velocities — each observer has their own frame of reference and the second observer's motion is described relative to that of the first. Einstein famously worked

A **null** result occurs when no relationship is observed between the variables in an experiment — in this case the speed of light and the existence of the æther.

Knowledge check 38

What was the æther?

Knowledge check 39

Why was it important to rotate the apparatus in Michelson and Morley's experiment?

Einstein's theory of **special relativity** refers to the motion of objects, notably at high speeds, moving at constant velocities relative to each other.

An **inertial frame of reference** is one in which all the objects within the frame are moving at the same velocity — in other words, they are all stationary relative to each other.

out the principles while sitting on trains during his daily commute to Zurich where he worked. He compared what he could see from the moving train (one frame of reference) to what people on the platform could see (a second frame of reference).

Einstein proposed two postulates to underpin his theory of special relativity:

1 Physical laws have the same form in all inertial frames.
2 The speed of light in free space is **invariant**.

Special relativity is a powerful theory and is particularly useful when explaining the behaviour of objects travelling at high speeds, such as the increase in the half-life of **muons** when they are travelling close to the speed of light compared to when they are static in the laboratory (known as time dilation), or the apparent shrinking of objects such as spacecraft as they are observed from Earth (called length contraction).

Time dilation

Special relativity shows us that, just as there is no fixed reference point that we can gauge movement from, there is no measure of absolute time that we can measure events against.

This is best shown using an example. Two astronauts, Anna and Beth, are travelling parallel to each other in space. Beth is in a spacecraft and Anna is on a space station. Beth has two parallel mirrors, a distance L apart, and a clock on board her spacecraft to measure the time taken for a pulse of light to travel from one mirror to the other and then back again. This is shown in Figure 31(a).

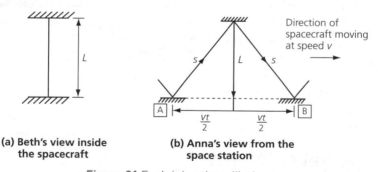

(a) Beth's view inside the spacecraft

(b) Anna's view from the space station

Figure 31 Explaining time dilation

From inside the space station, Anna sees the beam of light on Beth's spacecraft travel a different path because Beth's spacecraft is moving relative to the space station at speed v. During the time that the light beam is travelling, the two mirrors change position, relative to Anna, as shown in Figure 31(b). The nearest mirror moves from A to B and the furthest mirror is at the position shown in Figure 31(b) when the beam reflects from it. Anna times how long it takes for the beam to move between the mirrors, as seen from the space station, using a clock on board the space station. You can see that if the beam of light travels at the speed of light, the light appears to travel a further distance in (b) than it does in (a). The two clocks will not read the same time interval and Anna will measure a longer time than Beth.

The speed of light is 'invariant' means that i is always the same, no matter where or how you 'measure it.

Muons are fundamenta particles, part of the lepton family — similar to electrons but much more massive.

Knowledge check 40

What were Einstein's two postulates of special relativity?

nside the spacecraft, Beth sees that the light travels a distance $2L$. She measures he time taken as $2L/c$, where c is the speed of light in a vacuum. This is called the proper time, t_0.

$$t_0 = \frac{2L}{c}$$

On board the space station, Anna sees that the light has travelled further. Using Pythagoras' theorem, the distance the light travels is $2s$, where:

$$s = \sqrt{L^2 + \frac{v^2 t^2}{4}}$$

Rearranging this equation and substituting the proper time, t_0, as measured by Beth, the time, t, measured by Anna is given by:

$$t = \frac{t_0}{\sqrt{1 - \frac{v^2}{c^2}}}$$

Because v is always slower than c for an object, t is always longer than t_0. In other words, objects moving at speed, relative to an observer, have longer 'event' times — this is known as **time dilation**.

An example of time dilation is the increase of the half-life of muons when they are travelling at speeds close to the speed of light through the upper atmosphere of the Earth. In a laboratory on Earth, muons have a half-life of 1.56 μs, and in the upper atmosphere muons are observed to be moving at 0.98c. The high speed of the muons means that the half-life of muons moving in the upper atmosphere is:

$$t = \frac{1.56 \times 10^{-6}\,\text{s}}{\sqrt{1 - \frac{(0.98c)^2}{c^2}}} = 7.84\,\mu\text{s}$$

As a consequence of this, we get about 160 times more muons hitting the Earth than we would expect if their half-life was only 1.56 μs.

Length contraction

Using a reasoning similar to time dilation, the **proper length** of an object (for example a long straight rod, as measured by Beth on her spacecraft) is l_0 — i.e. its length as measured by an observer at rest relative to the rod. If the rod is moving parallel to an observer (e.g. Anna) with velocity v, then the time measured by Anna (on the space station) for the rod to pass her is t_0 (Anna is at rest with respect to her clock) so the length of the rod as measured by Anna is $l = vt_0$.

Exam tip

Use t_0 for the time that Anna measures because she is the person who is in the same frame of reference as her clock.

For Beth, the proper length of the rod, l_0, is equal to vt. Combining these equations and substituting for the time dilation equation we get the **length contraction** given by:

$$l = l_0 \sqrt{1 - \frac{v^2}{c^2}}$$

The **proper time** is the time, t_0, measured by an observer in the same frame of reference as the event that is being timed.

Time dilation is the observation that time, in a frame of reference moving relative to another frame of reference, appears to run more slowly in the *moving* frame of reference.

Knowledge check 41

Calculate the distance travelled by muons through the top of the atmosphere during one half-life travelling at 0.98c, if the half-lives of the muons are 1.56 μs and 7.84 μs respectively.

The **proper length** of an object is its length as measured by an observer in the same inertial reference frame as the object.

Length contraction is the observation that objects in a frame of reference moving relative to an observer's frame of reference appear to be shorter than objects in the observer's frame of reference.

Content Guidance

Knowledge check 42

Calculate the length of a spacecraft antenna, as seen from a nearby space station, if the spacecraft is travelling at 0.2c with respect to the space station. The antenna is measured to be 6.8m long using a tape measure on the spacecraft.

Mass and energy

Einstein also showed that mass has relativistic effects. The proper mass, m_0, of an object is the mass of the object at rest in its frame of reference — also called its **rest mass**. This gives rise to a rest energy, $E = m_0c^2$, and a relativistic energy, $E = mc^2$.

Due to special relativity, and similar explanations for time dilation and length contraction, the relationship between **relativistic energy, E**, and the rest mass of an object, m_0, measured by an observer in a different frame of reference moving at a velocity, v, relative to it is given by:

$$E = \frac{m_0c^2}{\sqrt{1-\dfrac{v^2}{c^2}}}$$

As the velocity of an object increases, the consequences are:

- its mass increases (as measured by an observer)
- it requires more energy to increase the velocity of the object

Figure 32 shows a graph of the ratio of mass/relativistic mass (m/m_0) against velocity (in units of c). You can see that at low velocities ($v \ll c$) the effects of relativity are very small and (m/m_0) = 1.

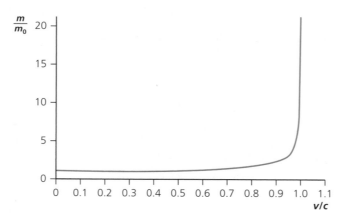

Figure 32 The change in relativistic mass with velocity

Figure 33 shows the change in energy (in terms of rest mass) of an object as its velocity (in units of c) increases. At $v = 0$ the energy is the energy equivalent of the rest mass, $E = m_0c^2$.

Exam tip

Length contraction only occurs when the distances measured are parallel to the direction of travel. Distances at right angles to the motion do not change.

The **rest mass** of an object is its mass measured by an observer moving in the same frame of reference as the object — i.e. at rest relative to the object.

The **relativistic energy** of an object is its energy measured by an observer in a different frame of reference.

Exam tip

Relativity only seems to become important at velocities of about 50% of c.

Knowledge check 43

What are the consequences of the relativistic mass equation?

40 AQA Physics

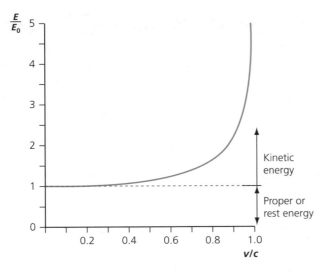

Figure 33 A graph showing how the energy of an object changes as it moves at higher velocities

As the speed increases, from about $v = 0.5c$, the relativistic mass starts to increase relative to the rest mass. At $v = 0.9c$ the relativistic mass is about 2.5 times that of the rest mass.

Einstein's equations were tested directly in 1964 when William Bertozzi published a paper that reported experiments using an electron accelerator to accelerate electrons to speeds close to the speed of light. In each of his experiments, electrons travelled a distance of 8.4 m until they crashed into an aluminium target. The time-of-flight of the electrons was measured and the velocity data agreed with Einstein's relativistic equations. Bertozzi also measured the thermal energy released when the electrons hit the aluminium target, from which he calculated their kinetic energy. Bertozzi's results were within 10% of the relativistic predictions of the kinetic energy of the electrons. A graph showing Bertozzi's results and the predictions from relativity theory is shown in Figure 34.

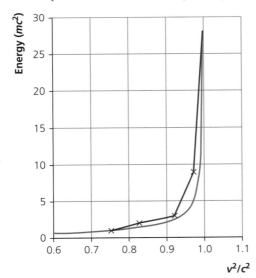

Figure 34 Bertozzi's electron energy data (blue) and the relativistic predictions (green)

Content Guidance

Summary

- The Michelson–Morley experiment provided evidence for the non-existence of Huygens' æther and, as such, the ability to detect absolute motion. In the absence of absolute motion, the motion of an object is therefore relative to the motion of other objects.
- The principle of operation of the Michelson–Morley interferometer is shown in Figure 30.
- Michelson and Morley's experiment gave direct observation of the fact that the speed of light is invariant.
- Einstein's theory of special relativity considers the motion of objects moving relative to one another at a constant velocity.
- An inertial frame of reference is one in which all objects within the frame of reference are moving at the same velocity and are effectively stationary with respect to each other. Objects moving at different velocities have different inertial reference frames, and the motion of one object is analysed with respect to the other.
- Einstein's theory of special relativity has two postulates:
  - Physical laws have the same form in all inertial frames.
  - The speed of light in free space is invariant.
- As a consequence of special relativity, time for an object moving at high velocity relative to a second object appears to go more slowly when observed from the second object. Time for the second object is called the proper time, t_0, and the time dilation on the first object is given by t. These two quantities are related to each other by the equation:

$$t = \frac{t_0}{\sqrt{1 - \dfrac{v^2}{c^2}}}$$

- Good evidence for time dilation comes from the change in the half-life of muons in cosmic rays high up in the Earth's atmosphere. Muons moving at $0.98c$ have a half-life of $7.84\,\mu s$ whereas muons at rest in a laboratory frame of reference have a half-life of $1.56\,\mu s$.
- A second consequence of special relativity is that objects moving at high velocities relative to an observer appear to get shorter — this is called length contraction:

$$l = l_0\sqrt{1 - \frac{v^2}{c^2}}$$

where l_0 is the proper length of the object in its inertial reference frame and l is the contracted length measured from a different frame of reference.
- The energy of an object moving at high velocity is subject to relativistic effects. The relativistic energy of an object is given by:

$$E = \frac{m_0 c^2}{\sqrt{1 - \dfrac{v^2}{c^2}}}$$

where m_0 is the rest mass of the object.
- Graphs of the variation of mass and kinetic energy with velocity are shown in Figures 32 and 33.
- Bertozzi's experiments provided direct evidence for the variation of kinetic energy with speed.

Questions & Answers

The content of this book is assessed in Paper 3, Section B of the A-level papers. Paper 3 is allocated 2 hours, contains 80 marks and is worth 32% of the A-level qualification. Section A is compulsory and examines practical skills and data analysis from Sections 1 to 8 of the specification. It has 45 marks in short- and longer-answer questions on practical experiments and data analysis. Section A of this paper is **not** covered by this book. Section B has 35 marks in short- and longer-answer questions on **one** optional topic — Astrophysics; Medical physics; Engineering physics; Turning points in physics; and Electronics. The Astrophysics and Turning points in physics topics are covered by this book. Section B assumes knowledge of the rest of the specification.

The following two test papers are made up of questions that are similar in style and content to those in the A-level examinations. There are 10 questions in both tests and they are a mixture of short- and longer-answer questions. The number of marks for each question are indicated next to the question. You should spend approximately 2½ hours on each test. Any data you need can be looked up in the AQA A-level Physics data booklet (http://aqa.org.uk/resources/physics/AQA-7408-SDB.pdf).

Although these sample questions resemble actual examination scripts, be aware that during the examination you will be writing your answers directly on the examination paper, which is not possible for this book. It may be that you will need to copy diagrams and graphs that you would normally just write or draw on in the real examination — if you are doing these tests under timed circumstances, you need to allow extra time for this.

Each question has some form of guidance. This could be hints on how to answer the questions; a clear statement about what the question is about; suggested content to revisit; or it could take the form of help on the mark schemes; pointing out common mistakes or giving suggestions about things to learn. The student answers consist of the correct answers and ✓ marks to show where marks are awarded. For many of the answers there is guidance showing the grade an answer might be awarded.

■Test paper 1: Astrophysics

Question 1

(a) Draw a ray diagram showing how a diminished image of a real object can be formed by a converging lens. You should label the object, image and principal foci of the lens on your diagram.

(3 marks)

(b) A converging lens has a focal length of approximately 50 cm. A student fixed an object 200 cm from a screen. When the lens was 128 cm from the object she could see a sharp image on the screen. Calculate the focal length of the converging lens.

(2 marks)

(c) The lens in part (b) was used as one of the lenses in a simple refracting astronomical telescope. State if the lens was the eyepiece or the objective lens in the telescope, giving reasons for your answer.

(2 marks)

Answer

(a)

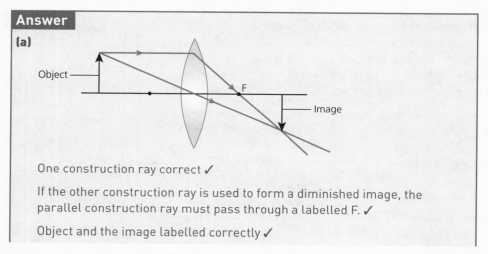

One construction ray correct ✓

If the other construction ray is used to form a diminished image, the parallel construction ray must pass through a labelled F. ✓

Object and the image labelled correctly ✓

e (C grade) The arrowheads on the lines are not essential. The construction ray must have a labelled focus to get the mark. You would lose the second mark if the image is the same size or magnified.

(b) $u = 128$ cm; $v = 200 - 128 = 72$ cm ✓

Use of $1/f = 1/u + 1/v$ to give $1/f = 1/128 + 1/72$; $f = 46$ cm ✓

e (A/B grade) If you calculate the value of v incorrectly but then correctly use your value of v to calculate f, you would get 1 mark. You must get v and u the correct way round.

(c) Objective lens

Magnification $M = f_o/f_e$, so magnification occurs where $f_o > f_e$ ✓

Telescope length $= f_o + f_e$, so the lens must be the objective lens (so that the telescope is not too long). ✓

⊜ (C grade) You would not get either mark if your answer is unsupported by an explanation.

Question 2

a) Table 1 shows some of properties of two stars in the constellation of Cetus.

Table 1

Name	Apparent magnitude	Radius of star/radius of Sun	Spectral class
Alpha	2.0	50	F
Beta	2.0	50	K

(i) Using these data, describe and explain *one* similarity and *one* difference in the appearance of the two stars as seen from Earth by an astronomer with the unaided eye. (2 marks)

(ii) State and explain which of the two stars is further from Earth. (3 marks)

b) Cetus also contains the galaxy NGC 2564. Measurements indicate that the light from the galaxy has a redshift, z, of 0.025 and that the galaxy is 340 million light years from Earth.

(i) Using these data, calculate a value for the Hubble constant. (3 marks)

(ii) Using your answer to part (b)(i), estimate a value for the age of the Universe and give an appropriate unit for your answer. (3 marks)

Answer

(a) (i) Similarity — both would appear the same brightness because the apparent magnitudes are the same. ✓

Difference — Beta would appear orange/red and Alpha yellow/white because they have different spectral classes/different temperatures. ✓

⊜ (C grade) You must give a description and an explanation for each mark. You would not get any marks for reference to the fact that they are the same size. You can state that they have different temperatures for the second mark (if qualified by an explanation).

(a) (ii) Alpha is further from Earth.

Both stars are the same size (with surface area A) and Alpha is hotter. ✓

The output power of a star is given by $P = \sigma A T^4$.

Because they both have the same A, this means that Alpha has the higher power output. ✓

So Alpha must be further from Earth to appear the same brightness as Beta. ✓

ℯ (A/B grade) An alternative approach to this answer is to state that Alpha is hotter and the same size.

Hence, Alpha has a brighter absolute magnitude and so it is intrinsically brighter. ✓

Because they have the same apparent brightness, Alpha is further away. ✓

(b) (i) $v = Hd$ so $v = 0.025 \times 3 \times 10^5 = 7.5 \times 10^3 \, \text{km s}^{-1}$ ✓

$d = 340 \times 10^6 \, \text{ly} = 340/3.26 \, \text{Mpc} = 104 \, \text{Mpc}$ ✓

Hence, $H = 7.5 \times 10^3/104 = 72 \, \text{km s}^{-1} \, \text{Mpc}^{-1}$ ✓

ℯ (A/B grade) The first mark is for calculating v; the second is for working out d in Mpc; the third is for calculating H and stating the correct unit.

(b) (ii) The age of the Universe is given by $T = 1/H$. ✓

$T = 0.014 \times 10^6 \times 3.26 \times 9.5 \times 10^{15}/1000 = 4.3 \times 10^{17} \, \text{s}$ ✓

So $T = 13.7$ billion years (the unit 'years' is consistent with the calculation). ✓

ℯ (A/B grade) The first mark is for the equation; the second is for the answer with working; the third is for a time unit consistent with the answer/working.

Question 3

(a) Draw a ray diagram for an astronomical refracting telescope in normal adjustment. Your diagram should show the paths of three non-axial rays passing through both lenses. Label the principal foci of the two lenses. (3 marks)

(b) The Barrow Telescope is one of the longest refracting telescopes in Europe. Some of its properties are summarised below:

- objective lens to eyepiece lens distance = 21 m
- angular magnification = 210
- diameter of the objective lens = 0.68 m

(i) Calculate the focal lengths of the objective lens and the eyepiece lens in the Barrow Telescope. (2 marks)

(ii) Early telescopes had very small-diameter objective lenses. State *two* advantages of using an astronomical telescope that has a large-diameter objective lens when making observations (2 marks)

c) Refracting telescopes suffer from chromatic aberration, degrading the quality of the images formed. Draw a labelled diagram showing how chromatic aberration is caused by a converging lens.

(1 mark)

Answer

(a)

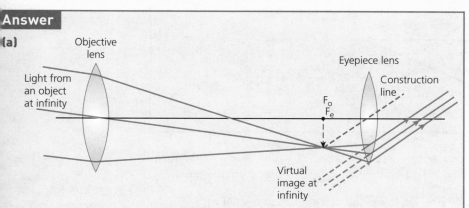

Both focal lengths to be labelled, also coinciding with each other on the principal axis, with $f_o > f_e$. ✓

Three off-axis rays going through the objective lens correctly. ✓

Three rays going through the eyepiece correctly and drawn parallel to a construction line. ✓

e (C grade) You can have the focal points or the focal lengths labelled for 1 mark. You can also have a single focal point labelled F for 1 mark. The rays must be off-axis to get the second mark. You do not have to have a construction line for 1 mark. If you have drawn only two rays, or you have not drawn a principal axis, maximum 2 marks.

(b) (i) Using $f_o + f_e = 21$ and $f_o/f_e = 210$ ✓
gives $211f_e = 21$, so $f_e = 21/211 = 0.10\,m$ and $f_o = 21\,m$ (20.9) ✓

e (A/B grade) You must give evidence of both equations for the first mark.

(b) (ii) The larger diameter allows the imaging of fainter objects (because the collecting power is proportional to d^2). ✓
The larger diameter gives much better angular resolution (because the smallest resolvable angle is proportional to $1/d$). ✓

e (C grade) You can state that: more light is collected (or better collecting power); or there is a brighter image formed; or you are able to see more (distant) objects but not see further. You can also make reference to more detail or clearer images to get this mark. You cannot get the marks if you give references to magnification or field of vision.

(c)

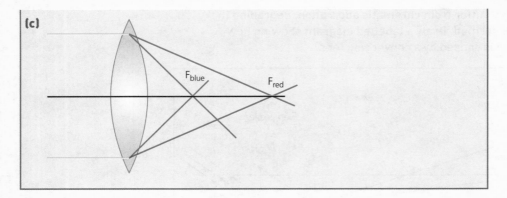

ⓔ You need to draw a diagram showing two focal points — one blue with the focal point closer to the lens; and one red with the focal point further from the lens.

(C grade) The colours must be labelled to get the mark. You could label with wavelengths or frequencies provided they are correct. The rays must be focused. You can have one ray for each colour if you have a principal axis drawn and the foci labelled. If you have included any other colours they must be in the correct order. You can have violet for blue. The incident rays do not need to be parallel to the principal axis.

Question 4

(a) Define the term 'absolute magnitude'. (1 mark)

(b) Figure 1 shows the labelled axes of a Hertzsprung–Russell diagram. Make a copy of Figure 1 and add suitable scales for both axes. (2 marks)

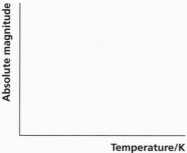

Figure 1

(c) Label a possible position of each of the following stars on your diagram:

    (i) the Sun (1 mark)

    (ii) a star labelled P, which has the same intrinsic brightness as the Sun, but a much higher temperature (1 mark)

    (iii) a star labelled Q, which has a similar spectrum to the Sun but is much larger (1 mark)

    (iv) a star labelled R, which is much larger than the Sun and has prominent spectral absorption lines of neutral atoms and titanium oxide (TiO). (1 mark)

(d) State and explain how the diameter of star P (in part (c)(ii)) compares with the diameter of the Sun. (3 marks)

Answer

(a) The apparent magnitude at a distance of 10 pc ✓

ⓔ (C grade) You can have 'brightness' instead of apparent magnitude, but you cannot have 'luminosity' or 'magnitude'.

(b) The absolute magnitude scale goes from 15 to –10. ✓

The temperature scale goes from 50 000 K to 2500 K. ✓

ⓔ (C grade) You can have the values 15 to –15 and 50 000 K to 3500 K.

(c) (i) The Sun must be labelled at 5700 K and absolute magnitude of 5. ✓

ⓔ (C grade) The position of the Sun label should be consistent with the scales on each axis. If there are no labels on the axes, or if there are only correct extreme values, the Sun label should be to the right of and below the centre of the diagram.

(c) (ii) P should be at the same absolute magnitude as the Sun, but further to the left on the diagram. ✓

ⓔ (C grade) The marks awarded for parts (c)(ii) to (iv) should be determined relative to the position of the Sun on the diagram. If the Sun is not labelled, they should be based on where the Sun should be.

(c) (iii) The position of Q should be at the same temperature as the Sun but have a higher absolute magnitude. ✓

(iv) The position of R should be at the same absolute magnitude as or above that of the Sun, and on the right-hand side of the diagram. ✓

(d) P should have a similar power output to the Sun ✓ but it is hotter. ✓

The power emitted by the star is given by σAT^4, so P must have a smaller diameter than the Sun. ✓

Question 5

Aquilla A is a quasar that may be the closest quasar yet discovered.

(a) The redshift, z, of Aquilla A is 0.057. Calculate the distance to Aquilla A and give a suitable unit for your answer. (4 marks)

(b) State the property of quasars that led to their first discovery in the 1950s. (1 mark)

Answer

(a) Using $z = v/c$ gives $v = zc = 0.057 \times 3 \times 10^8$ ✓ $= 1.71 \times 10^7 \, \text{m s}^{-1} = 1.71 \times 10^4 \, \text{km s}^{-1}$

Then $v = Hd$ giving $d = v/H = 1.71 \times 10^4 \, / \, 65$ ✓ $= 263$ ✓ Mpc ✓

🅔 (A/B grade) Your answer can be stated in ly ($\times 3.26$) = 857 ly or metres ($\times 3.09 \times 10^{16}$) = 8.13×10^{18} m.

> **(b)** They are (strong) radio sources. ✓

🅔 (C grade) Your answer does not need to state categorically that they are strong sources.

Question 6

Centaurus A is the nearest example of an active galactic nucleus. Many astronomers believe that a supermassive black hole at the centre of such a galaxy produces a quasar as it consumes the material of its nearby stars.

(a) Explain what is meant by the 'event horizon' of a black hole. (1 mark)

(b) **(i)** The mass of the black hole is 60 million times the mass of the Sun. Calculate the radius of its event horizon. (2 marks)

(ii) Calculate the average density of the matter within its event horizon. (2 marks)

> **Answer**
>
> **(a)** The boundary around a black hole where the escape velocity is c. ✓

🅔 (C grade) No marks can be awarded for stating that the event horizon is a point.

> **(b) (i)** Using $R_s = 2GM/c^2$ gives $R_s = 2 \times 6.67 \times 10^{-11} \times 60 \times 10^6 \times 1.99 \times 10^{30} /$
> $(3 \times 10^8)^2$ ✓ $= 1.8 \times 10^{11}$ m ✓

🅔 (A/B grade) Don't forget to square the velocity of light.

> **(b) (ii)** Using $\rho = m/V$ gives $\rho = \dfrac{60 \times 10^6 \times 2 \times 10^{30}}{\left(\dfrac{4}{3} \pi \times \left(1.78 \times 10^{11} \right)^3 \right)}$ ✓ $= 5.1 \times 10^3$ kg m^{-3} ✓

🅔 (A/B grade) You must remember the formula for the volume of a sphere, or be able to find it in the data booklet.

Question 7

The European Space Agency X-ray telescope XMM-Newton was launched in 1999. Its mission is to observe high-energy events in energetic regions of the Universe.

(a) Explain why X-ray telescopes are put into orbit around the Earth. (1 mark)

(b) XMM-Newton is used to observe black holes.

(i) Explain what is meant by a black hole. (1 mark)

(ii) One black hole observed by the XMM-Newton telescope has a mass approximately eight times the mass of the Sun. Use these data to determine the radius of the event horizon of this black hole. (2 marks)

c) The XMM-Newton uses a charge-coupled device (CCD) X-ray imaging system. Describe how a CCD detects photons of electromagnetic energy. (3 marks)

Answer

(a) The Earth's atmosphere absorbs X-rays. ✓

(b) (i) A black hole is an object in space whose escape velocity is greater than the speed of light. ✓

(ii) The event horizon is defined by the Schwarzschild equation: $R_S = \dfrac{2GM}{c^2}$

Using data from the data booklet, where the mass of the Sun is given as 2.0×10^{30} kg:

$$R_S = \frac{2 \times 6.67 \times 10^{-11} \, \text{N m}^2 \, \text{kg}^{-2} \times 8 \times 2.0 \times 10^{30} \, \text{kg}}{\left(3.0 \times 10^8 \, \text{m s}^{-1}\right)^2} \checkmark$$

$$= 23\,716 \, \text{m} = 24\,000 \, \text{m} \, (2 \, \text{sf}) \checkmark$$

ℯ (A/B grade) Don't forget to use the same number of significant figures in your answer as the least significant data used.

(c) A CCD electronic detector consists of a silicon photon-sensitive surface. ✓ The incident photons cause electrons to be released from the structure, ✓ which are then trapped in potential wells inside the CCD. ✓

Question 8

In 1949, the British astronomer Fred Hoyle first used the term 'Big Bang' to describe the formation of the Universe. The Big Bang theory was not the only explanation for the formation of the Universe and Hoyle was the main opponent to the theory, preferring his 'steady-state' theory instead.

a) Describe and explain what is meant by the Big Bang theory. You should include in your answer:
- a description of the main aspects of the Big Bang theory
- an explanation of the different pieces of observational evidence that support the Big Bang theory.

You will be assessed on the quality of your written communication. (6 marks)

b) Modern telescopes have been able to detect an acceleration in the expansion of the Universe using observations from type 1a supernovae, which are used as standard candles.

(i) State the meaning of the term 'standard candle'. (1 mark)

(ii) Measurements made by direct observation of type 1a supernova can be used to calculate the distance of the supernova from Earth. Explain how this is done. (3 marks)

Questions & Answers

(e) The marks awarded for part (a) are determined by the quality of your written communication in addition to the standard of your scientific responses. Your answer is marked on a 'best-fit' basis assigning it to one of three levels using the criteria in the table below.

(A–E grade) Your handwriting should be legible (the examiner must be able to read it) and the spelling, punctuation and grammar should be good enough for the meaning of your answer to be clear. Your answer will be assessed holistically — this means that the examiner will read the answer completely first and then assign a mark based on the whole of your response.

0 marks	Level 1 (E grade) (1–2 marks)	Level 2 (C grade) (3–4 marks)	Level 3 (A grade) (5–6 marks)
No relevant content.	Lower level (poor to limited): 1 or 2 marks The information conveyed by your answer is poorly organised and may not be relevant or coherent. You have included little correct use of specialist vocabulary. The form and style of your writing may be only partly appropriate. You may not have explained what the Big Bang theory is. You may only have referred to one piece of evidence that supports the theory.	Intermediate level (modest to adequate): 3 or 4 marks The information conveyed by your answer may be less well organised and not fully coherent. You have less use of specialist vocabulary than for a high level answer, or you may have used the specialist vocabulary incorrectly. The form and style of your writing is less appropriate than for a high level answer. You may have only referred poorly to two pieces of supporting evidence or referred to one in detail and your description of the Big Bang theory may not be as complete as a high level answer.	High level (good to excellent): 5 or 6 marks The information conveyed by your answer is clearly organised, logical and coherent and uses appropriate specialist vocabulary correctly. The form and style of your writing is appropriate to answer the question. You have described the Big Bang theory as the Universe expanding from an extremely dense and hot point over the past 13.8 billion years. You have also described the evidence from the relative abundances of H and He and the measurement of the microwave background radiation and stated that they support the Big Bang theory. You may also have used Hubble's law to support the idea that the Universe is expanding.

A good answer should include most of the following physics ideas:

- The Universe has expanded from a single hot, dense point.
- The expansion of the Universe started approximately 14 billion years ago.
- Direct observational evidence for the Big Bang comes from the Hubble relationship and observations of the cosmological redshift of distant galaxies.
- The cosmological redshift shows that galaxies are moving outwards, away from a single common point.
- The best evidence comes from the cosmological microwave background radiation (CMBR) (which also disproved the steady-state theory).
- The CMBR follows a black-body radiation curve corresponding to a black body with a temperature of 2.7 K.
- The CMBR is interpreted as remnant 'heat' of the Big Bang.
- The ratio of hydrogen to helium present in the Universe is 3 : 1, supporting the idea that when the Universe was very young there was a brief period of nuclear fusion, which is consistent with the Big Bang theory.

(b) (i) A standard candle is an object (in the Universe emitting radiation, generally light) whose absolute magnitude is known. ✓

e (C grade) You would not get the mark if you use the term 'brightness' instead of 'absolute magnitude', although the term 'intrinsic brightness' is acceptable. You cannot use the word 'constant' to mean the word 'known'.

(b) (ii) Type 1a supernovae all have same peak absolute magnitude (which is known) when they explode. ✓

The apparent magnitude of the supernova can be measured at the peak of its emission. ✓

The equation $m - M = 5 \log_{10}\left(\dfrac{d}{10}\right)$ can then be used to determine d. ✓

(Or the inverse square law can be used to determine d.)

e (C grade) The alternative answer using the inverse square law is: All type 1a supernova have the same peak intensity of emission, I_0; the intensity of the radiation received on Earth can be measured, I; the distance, d, to the object can then be calculated using $= I_0/d^2$. If you do not refer to the peak of emissions you can only get a maximum of 2 marks.

Question 9

The CORALIE detector attached to the Leonhard Euler telescope is a system designed to detect exoplanets.

(a) The CORALIE detector uses a charge-coupled device (CCD) with a quantum efficiency of 96% for red light of wavelength 750 nm. Explain what is meant by the 'quantum efficiency' of a CCD.

(1 mark)

(b) (i) The Leonhard Euler telescope includes a curved objective mirror with a diameter of 0.60 m. Use this measurement to determine the minimum angular separation of two objects emitting red light of wavelength 750 nm that can be just resolved by this telescope.

(1 mark)

(ii) An exoplanet is observed to be 10.5 light years from Earth and orbits its star with an elliptical orbit varying between 1 AU and 5 AU. Determine the maximum angular separation of the star and the planet when viewed from Earth at a distance of 10.5 light years.

(3 marks)

(iii) The CORALIE/Euler telescope system detects exoplanets using the transit method by measuring the change of light intensity when the planet passes in front of the star. It is unlikely that the telescope will be able to observe exoplanets directly. Explain why this is the case.

(1 mark)

(c) Astronomers use a huge range of different types of telescope to observe objects in space at different wavelengths of the electromagnetic spectrum. Pick *three* different parts of the electromagnetic spectrum and discuss the factors that need to be taken into account when making a decision about the location and size of suitable telescopes. You will be assessed on the quality of your written communication as part of this answer.

(6 marks)

Answer

(a) The percentage of photons hitting the CCD that are detected and/or produce a signal. ✓

@ (C grade) You must refer to the photons incident on the CCD in your answer.

(b) (i) Use of $\theta = \lambda/D$ to give $\theta = 750 \times 10^{-9}/0.60 = 1.25 \times 10^{-6}$ (rad) ✓

@ Beware of making careless mistakes such as inverting the values when substituting into the equation, or incorrectly converting nanometres to metres.

(b) (ii) Use of $s = r\theta$ to give $\theta = (5 \times 1.5 \times 10^{11})$ ✓$/(10.5 \times 9.46 \times 10^{15})$ ✓
   $= 7.55 \times 10^{-6}$ ✓ (rad)

@ (A/B grade) You must be able to convert the two distances into the same unit — conversion factors are given in the data booklet. Remember that the unit of angle in this case is the radian.

(b) (iii) Either answer (b)(i) is a theoretical limit — and in reality the resolving power will be much poorer than this (due to atmosphere, etc.) — or the planets will be far too dim to see (next to the star). ✓

@ (C grade) The angular resolution of the telescope is lower than the angular separation of the planet and star, so the telescope should be able to see it, unless the light intensity from the star is too low.

@ (A–E grade) For part (c) your handwriting should be easy to read and your spelling, punctuation and grammar need to be suitably accurate for the examiner to understand the meaning clearly.

Your answer will be assessed as a whole and needs to be put into one of three tiered levels according to the following criteria.

High level (good to excellent): 5 or 6 marks

Your answer is clearly organised, logical and coherent and uses appropriate specialist vocabulary correctly. The form and style of your writing is appropriate to answer the question.

Your answer gives a comprehensive and logical explanation that considers the detection of three named parts of the electromagnetic spectrum. Your answer describes how the optimum siting of a telescope is determined by the effect of the atmosphere and, for full marks, you have considered the effect that other factors (such as light pollution) have on the three named parts of the electromagnetic spectrum. Your answer also demonstrates an understanding of how resolving power, and for (full marks) the collecting power of a telescope, is affected by the size of the aperture, and relates the resolving power to the wavelengths of the three different parts of the electromagnetic spectrum.

Intermediate level (modest to adequate): 3 or 4 marks

Your answer may be less-well organised and not fully coherent. You have used less specialist vocabulary, or the specialist vocabulary that you have used may be used incorrectly. The form and style of writing in your answer is less appropriate.

Your answer has given a comprehensive and logical explanation and names two or three parts of the electromagnetic spectrum and has included a discussion about both telescope siting and size for at least two of the parts of the electromagnetic spectrum for 4 marks, or for 3 marks only one of them. Your answer may show that you recognise that some telescopes need to be in orbit because of the absorption of some parts of the electromagnetic spectrum by the atmosphere. You may also have discussed the siting of telescopes — for example telescopes should be at higher altitudes to reduce the absorption of infrared radiation. Your answer may refer to only one of resolving power or collecting power when discussing the size of telescopes, and for 3 marks there may be minimal or no attempt to relate resolving power to wavelength.

Low level (poor to limited): 1 or 2 marks

Your answer is poorly organised and may not be relevant or coherent. You may have used limited specialist vocabulary correctly. The form and style of writing in your answer may be only partly appropriate.

Your answer recognises that some telescopes are in orbit, and for 2 marks you may have described a part of the electromagnetic spectrum being detected. Your answer may be confused about which parts of the electromagnetic spectrum are absorbed by the atmosphere and which pass through. For 2 marks your answer may include a vague reference to the size of telescopes, and for 1 mark your answer may have no reference at all to size.

A good answer should include the following points to support your explanation:

Siting

- All parts of the electromagnetic spectrum, with the exception of visible and some parts of radio wave, are significantly absorbed by the atmosphere.
- Infrared telescopes are usually sited in dry/high locations to reduce the effects of absorption.

- The ozone layer of the atmosphere absorbs ultraviolet radiation significantly and, as such, ultraviolet telescopes are usually put into orbit.
- X-ray telescopes and gamma-ray telescopes are put into orbit to avoid absorption by the atmosphere.
- Visible telescopes are generally put in high/dry/remote locations to reduce atmospheric distortion and light pollution from centres of population.
- Radio telescopes are usually put in locations away from centres of population to avoid interference from terrestrial radio and television signals.

Size

- Telescopes are generally designed to have the largest aperture possible to increase their collecting power, which is proportional to the square of the diameter.
- Telescopes are designed to have the largest objective diameter possible to increase the resolving power, because the minimum angle that can be resolved by the telescope is proportional to 1/diameter.

(A to E grade) You must answer the question correctly by writing about three parts of the electromagnetic spectrum, and you must refer to siting and size.

Question 10

One form of the Hertzsprung–Russell (HR) diagram plots the absolute magnitude of stars against their spectral class, and illustrates the similarities and differences between the main groups of stars.

(a) Sketch an example of this type of HR diagram with the absolute magnitude on the *y*-axis and the spectral class (OBAFGKM) on the *x*-axis. On the diagram label the main sequence stars, giant stars and white dwarf stars, and add a suitable absolute magnitude scale.   (3 marks)

(b) Polaris, the Pole Star, is the brightest star in the constellation of Ursa Minor and is actually an F class yellow supergiant star (Aa) with two smaller F class main sequence companions (Ab and Ac) forming what is called a ternary system.

    (i) The black-body radiation curve of the yellow supergiant Polaris Aa has a peak radiation wavelength of 485 nm. Use this information to calculate the black-body temperature of Polaris Aa to an appropriate number of significant figures.   (3 marks)

    (ii) The luminosity of Polaris Aa is 2500 times that of our Sun. If the surface temperature of our Sun is 5700 K, calculate the radius of Polaris Aa.   (3 marks)

(c) The A class star Vega has a spectrum dominated by hydrogen Balmer absorption lines. Describe how these absorption lines are formed in the spectrum of Vega. The quality of your written communication will be assessed in this question.   (6 marks)

Answer

(a) Absolute magnitude

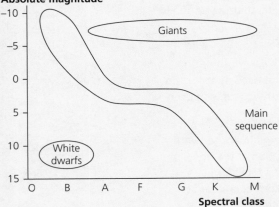

Plotting the main sequence curvature correctly. ✓

Plotting the giants and (white) dwarfs correctly. ✓

Labelling the absolute magnitude scale correctly (from 15 to −10). ✓

(b) (i) Using Wien's displacement law:

$$\lambda_{max}T = 0.0029 \, \text{m K} \checkmark$$

gives:

$$T = \frac{0.0029 \, \text{m K}}{4.85 \times 10^{-7} \, \text{m}} \checkmark$$

$$= 5.98 \times 10^3 \, \text{K} \checkmark$$

e (E grade) Remember to convert nm to m.

(b) (ii) Using Stefan's law:

$$\frac{P_P}{P_S} = \frac{\sigma A_P T_P^4}{\sigma A_S T_S^4}$$

giving:

$$\frac{A_P}{A_S} = \frac{P_P T_S^4}{P_S T_P^4}$$

$$\frac{A_P}{A_S} = 2500 \times \left(\frac{5700}{5980}\right)^4$$

$$= 2063 \checkmark$$

so:

$$\frac{r_P}{r_S} = \sqrt{2063} = 45.4 \checkmark$$

giving:

$$r_P = 45.4 \times 6.96 \times 10^8 \, \text{m} = 3.16 \times 10^{10} \, \text{m} \checkmark$$

ⓔ (A–E grade) For part (c) your handwriting should be legible and the spelling, punctuation and grammar should be good enough for the meaning to be clear.

Your answer will be assessed as a whole answer and needs to be assigned to one of three levels according to the following criteria.

High level (good to excellent): 5 or 6 marks

Your answer is clearly organised, logical and coherent and uses appropriate specialist vocabulary correctly. The form and style of your writing is appropriate to answer the question.

Your answer states that the atmosphere of the star contains hydrogen with electrons in the $n = 2$ state and it includes a clear description of the absorption process in the atmosphere of the star, with reference to energy jumps corresponding to specific frequencies of light. It also describes at least one reason for the gap in the spectrum in terms of the de-excitation process.

Intermediate level (modest to adequate): 3 or 4 marks

Your answer may be less well organised and not fully coherent. You have used less specialist vocabulary, or the specialist vocabulary that you have used may be used incorrectly. The form and style of your writing is less appropriate (than for a 5 or 6 mark answer).

Your answer may not state that electrons start in the $n = 2$ state. It may only include a satisfactory description of either excitation or de-excitation. Your answer includes some link between energy and frequency and there may be a clear reference to $E = hf$.

Low level (poor to limited): 1 or 2 marks

Your answer is poorly organised and may not be relevant or coherent. You have used limited specialist vocabulary correctly. The form and style of writing in your answer may be only partly appropriate.

Your answer recognises that changes in electron energy levels are involved but it may confuse absorption for emission, and the explanation of why the frequency of the light is important may be vague. There may also be confusion between absorption due to the star's atmosphere and the Earth's atmosphere.

A competent answer includes some of the following statements as marking points:

- The atmosphere of the star has hydrogen atoms with electrons in the $n = 2$ state.
- Light from the star passes through the atmosphere of the star.
- Electrons (in the $n = 2$ state) are excited into higher energy states.
- They can only absorb certain amounts of energy.
- These certain energies are related to specific frequencies ($E = hf$).
- The electrons then de-excite.
- The electrons may de-excite through different energy level changes.
- When the electrons de-excite, the light is radiated in all directions.
- This means that the intensity of the light at particular frequencies is reduced, resulting in absorption lines.

Test paper 2: Turning points in physics

Question 1

Figure 1 is a circuit diagram showing light of a given frequency incident on a metal surface in a vacuum photocell. Photoelectrons are emitted by the metal surface and are collected by electrode X inside the photocell.

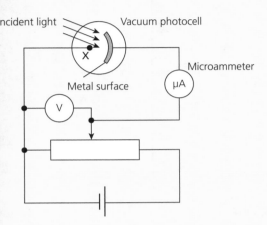

Figure 1

(a) The potential difference between the metal surface and electrode X can be changed by adjusting the potential divider. Explain why the reading on the microammeter decreases when the metal surface is made more positive relative to X.   (3 marks)

(b) The minimum potential difference applied between the metal surface and X to reduce the photoelectric current to zero when monochromatic light hits the metal surface is called the stopping potential, V_s. The circuit in Figure 1 is used, together with different frequencies of light, to measure stopping potentials when the surface is illuminated by different frequencies of light.

(i) Figure 2 shows the axes of a graph to show how V_s varies with the frequency, f, of the incident light. On a copy of Figure 2, sketch the graph you would expect to see.   (2 marks)

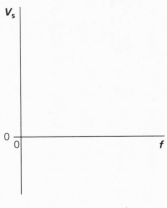

Figure 2

(ii) Use Einstein's photoelectric equation $hf = \phi + E_{kmax}$ to explain the shape of your graph. (3 marks)

(c) The photocell in Figure 1 was illuminated with purple light of wavelength 418 nm. A student measured the stopping potential to be 1.92 V. Use these data to calculate the work function of the metal surface. You must give a suitable unit in your answer. (4 marks)

> ### Answer
>
> (a) The emitted (photo) electrons have a range of speeds. ✓
>
> The (electrostatic) force acting on the photoelectrons emitted from the surface increases (or the pull/attraction on the photoelectrons from the surface increases). ✓
>
> The microammeter indicates the current due to photoelectrons reaching electrode X (which then move round the circuit). ✓
>
> (The current indicated on the microammeter decreases because) the photoelectrons are unable to reach X because of the increased force (or they do not have enough kinetic energy or there is too much work needed). ✓

ⓔ (A/B grade) There is an alternative answer for the last point — the current indicated by the microammeter decreases because fewer photoelectrons can reach electrode X as the PD increases.

> (b) (i) The graph should be a straight line with a positive gradient. ✓
> There should be an intercept on the positive x-axis (or the negative y-axis if drawn). ✓

ⓔ (C grade) You must have the first point in order to get the second point.

> (b) (ii) $E_{kmax} = eV_s$ ✓
> Therefore $eV_s = hf - \phi$, where hf is the energy of the incident photon and ϕ is the work function of the metal. ✓
> A graph of V_s against f will be a straight line with a gradient equal to h/e. ✓
> The x-intercept of the graph will be equal to ϕ/h (or the y-intercept will be equal to $-\phi/e$). ✓

ⓔ (A/B grade) There is an alternative for the second mark. $V_s = \dfrac{hf}{e} - \dfrac{\phi}{e}$ where ϕ is the work function of the metal. This is the equation for a straight line (or $y = mx + c$) graph. You can get the final 2 marks if the answers are shown clearly on the graph.

(c) $hf = \dfrac{6.63 \times 10^{-34}\,\text{Js} \times 3.0 \times 10^{8}\,\text{ms}^{-1}}{418 \times 10^{-9}\,\text{m}} = 4.76 \times 10^{-19}$ ✓

$E_{kmax} = eV_s = 1.6 \times 10^{-19}\,\text{C} \times 1.92\,\text{V} = 3.07 \times 10^{-19}\,\text{J}$ ✓

$\phi = hf - E_{kmax} = (4.76 \times 10^{-19} - 3.07 \times 10^{-19})\,\text{J} = 1.69 \times 10^{-19}$ ✓ J ✓ $\left(\text{or } 1.06\,\text{eV}\right)$

ⓔ (A/B grade) For the first 2 marks you could have just the numbers substituted into the (correct) equation. If your answer is given in J you could have 1.7, 1.70 or 1.66 (due to rounding) or if your answer is in eV you could have 1.1 or 1.04 (again due to rounding).

Question 2

(a) In Einstein's theory of special relativity, one of the postulates is that the laws of physics are the same in all inertial frames of reference. Explain in terms of velocity what is meant by an 'inertial frame of reference'.

(1 mark)

(b) Light from the star Proxima Centauri takes 4.3 years to reach the Earth.

(i) As measured by an observer on Earth, a spacecraft is to be sent from Earth to Proxima Centauri arriving after a trip time of 5.0 years. Calculate the speed (in ms^{-1}) of the spacecraft for this journey assuming that its velocity is constant for the whole journey.

(1 mark)

(ii) Calculate the trip time for this journey in years as measured by a clock on the spacecraft.

(3 marks)

Answer

(a) (A frame of reference that is) moving at a constant velocity. ✓

ⓔ (C grade) You could also say that it is a frame of reference that is not accelerating.

(b) (i) The distance travelled by the light is 4.3 light years, which is equal to $4.3 \times c = 4.1 \times 10^{16}\,\text{m}$.

The speed of the spacecraft is then given by:

$v = 4.3 \times c/5 = 0.86c = 2.6 \times 10^{8}\,\text{ms}^{-1}$ ✓

ⓔ (A/B grade) A value of 2.58×10^{8} is correct (due to rounding).

(b) (ii) $t = \dfrac{t_0}{\sqrt{1 - \dfrac{v^2}{c^2}}}$ where $t = 5.0$ years (or $1.58 \times 10^{8}\,\text{s}$) and $v = 0.86c$

(or $2.58 \times 10^{8}\,\text{ms}^{-1}$) ✓

e The first mark is for the correct substitution of either t or v into the time dilation equation.

Alternatively, you could answer using length contraction:

$$l = l_0 \sqrt{1 - \frac{v^2}{c^2}}$$

The first mark is for the correct substitution of either t or v into the length contraction equation.

$$l_0 = 4.3 \text{ y} \times 365 \text{ d} \times 24 \text{ h} \times 60 \text{ min} \times 60 \text{ s} \times 3.0 \times 10^8 \text{ ms}^{-1} = 4.07 \times 10^{16} \text{ m}$$

$$l = 4.07 \times 10^{16} \text{ m} \times \sqrt{1 - \frac{(0.86)^2}{c^2}} = 2.08 \times 10^{16} \text{ m} \checkmark$$

$$t_0 = \frac{l}{v} = \frac{2.08 \times 10^{16} \text{ m}}{2.6 \times 10^8 \text{ m s}^{-1}} = 8.05 \times 10^7 \text{ s} = 2.6 \text{ years} \checkmark$$

e (A/B grade) Using the time dilation method, you can have an error carried forward from (b)(i) to (b)(ii) provided your answer to (b)(i) is less than c. You can have t or v in any suitable (correct) units. You can have 1.58 (or 1.6) $\times 10^8$ s in place of 5.0 years for the third mark. The final answer can be any value between 2.5 and 2.6, given to any number of significant figures. Using the length contraction method, there is an alternative acceptable approach for the final 2 marks using light years where $l_0 = 4.3 \text{ ly}$:

$$l = 4.3 \text{ ly} \times \sqrt{1 - \frac{(0.86)^2}{c^2}} = 2.2 \text{ ly} \checkmark$$

$$\text{so } t_0 = \frac{l}{v} = \frac{2.2 \text{ ly}}{0.86c} = 2.6 \text{ y} \checkmark$$

Question 3

Figure 3 shows a charged oil droplet between two horizontal metal plates X and Y.

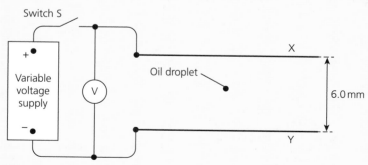

Figure 3

(a) (i) Switch S is initially open and the oil droplet is observed to fall vertically with a constant velocity of $1.1 \times 10^{-4}\,\text{m s}^{-1}$. Use a suitable equation to show that the radius of the oil droplet is about $1.0 \times 10^{-6}\,\text{m}$. (4 marks)

You can assume that the oil droplet is a sphere.

The viscosity of the air, η, is $1.8 \times 10^{-5}\,\text{N s m}^{-2}$.

The density of the oil, ρ, is $880\,\text{kg m}^{-3}$.

(ii) Calculate the mass of the oil droplet in kg. (1 mark)

(iii) Switch S is now closed. The motion of the oil droplet downwards is then reduced, so that the oil droplet stops moving, by adjusting the potential difference, V, from the variable voltage supply up to a value of 680 V. Calculate the size of the charge on the oil droplet if the gap between the metal plates is 6.0 mm. (3 marks)

(b) A second charged oil droplet was observed and its mass was measured to be $4.3 \times 10^{-15}\,\text{kg}$. The value of the potential difference across the plates was adjusted to its maximum of 1000 V, with switch S closed. The oil droplet fell more slowly than when the switch was open but it could not be made to stop falling. Show that the charge on this oil droplet was $1.6 \times 10^{-19}\,\text{C}$, and then explain why this oil droplet could not be held stationary. (4 marks)

Answer

(a) (i) (When travelling at its terminal velocity, v), the weight of the oil droplet (or mg) = the viscous drag on the oil droplet (or $6\pi\eta r v$) ✓

The mass of the oil droplet, $m = \left(\dfrac{4}{3}\pi r^3\right) \times \rho$, ($r$ is the radius of the oil droplet)

This means that $\left(\dfrac{4}{3}\pi r^3\right) \times \rho \times g = 6\pi\eta r v$ ✓

Therefore, $r = \sqrt{\dfrac{9\eta v}{2\rho g}}$ ✓ $= \sqrt{\dfrac{9 \times 1.8 \times 10^{-5}\,\text{N s m}^{-2} \times 1.1 \times 10^{-4}\,\text{m s}^{-1}}{2 \times 880\,\text{kg m}^{-3} \times 9.8\,\text{m s}^{-2}}}$

$= 1.0(2) \times 10^{-6}\,\text{m}$ ✓

ℯ You must have some evidence of a calculation in order to get the last mark.

(A/B grade) If you work backwards from the answer, the maximum mark you can get is 3. Your final numerical answer can be in the range of $1–1.05 \times 10^{-6}$ and can be to any number of significant figures (they are not marked as part of this answer).

(a) (ii) The mass of the oil droplet,

$m = \left(\dfrac{4}{3}\pi r^3\right) \times \rho = \left(\dfrac{4}{3}\pi \left(1.0 \times 10^{-6}\,\text{m}\right)^3\right) \times 880\,\text{kg m}^{-3} = 3.7 \times 10^{-15}\,\text{kg}$ ✓

ℯ (C grade) You can have an error carried forward from (a)(i) if the rest of the calculation is correct and provided m is in the range of $3.6–4.0 \times 10^{-15}\,\text{kg}$.

(a) (iii) The electric force exerted on the oil droplet (QV/d) is equal to the weight of the droplet (mg). ✓

So $Q = \dfrac{mgd}{V} = \dfrac{3.7 \times 10^{-15}\,\text{kg} \times 9.8\,\text{ms}^{-2} \times 6.0 \times 10^{-3}\,\text{m}}{680\,\text{V}}$ ✓ $= 3.2 \times 10^{-19}\,\text{C}$ ✓

ⓔ (C grade) You can have an error carried forward for your value of m (or r) from (a)(ii) or (a)(i). If you use the symbol e instead of Q (or q) you can get a maximum of only 2 marks.

(b) Any 4 of:

The maximum electric force acting on the second oil droplet must be lower than the weight of the oil droplet. ✓

(or weight of oil droplet = drag force acting on droplet + electric force on droplet)

If the second oil droplet has only one integer charge on it, the potential difference, V, required to hold it stationary is $mgd/e = 1580\,\text{V}$ ✓

This potential difference is not possible because the maximum available is 1000 V. ✓

If the oil droplet has two integer charges on it then $V = 790\,\text{V}$, and it would be held stationary by a potential of 790 V ($V = 1580/2$) ✓

If the droplet has more than two integer charges on it then it would be held stationary by less than 790 V ✓

This means that the charge on the droplet must be equal to $1e$. ✓

ⓔ (A/B grade) Remember that the oil droplet can only have integer values of charge e.

Question 4

(a) State the de Broglie hypothesis. (2 marks)

(b) A narrow beam of neutrons can show wave-like behaviour by diffracting via the atoms inside a crystal. If the neutrons have a kinetic energy, E_k, equal to 0.021 eV, calculate their de Broglie wavelength giving your answer in metres to a suitable number of significant figures. (4 marks)

(c) If a beam of electrons has the same de Broglie wavelength as the neutrons in part (b), they will have much more kinetic energy than 0.021 eV. Explain why this is the case. You can assume that relativistic effects are negligible. (2 marks)

Answer

(a) Particles can have wave-like properties ✓ and they have a de Broglie wavelength $\lambda = h/p$, where p is the momentum of the particles. ✓

ⓔ (C grade) You can have mv or mass × velocity instead of p.

(b) The kinetic energy of the neutrons is $E_k = 0.021\,\text{eV}$
$= 0.021\,\text{eV} \times 1.60 \times 10^{-19}\,\text{J} = 3.36 \times 10^{-21}\,\text{J}$ ✓

Rearranging the equation for kinetic energy to get momentum:

$$E_k = \frac{1}{2}mv^2 \Rightarrow mv = \sqrt{2mE_k} = \sqrt{2 \times 1.67 \times 10^{-27}\,\text{kg} \times 3.36 \times 10^{-21}\,\text{J}}$$

$$= 3.35 \times 10^{-24}\,\text{kg m s}^{-1}$$

Substituting into the de Broglie equation:

$$\lambda = \frac{h}{mv} = \frac{6.63 \times 10^{-34}\,\text{J s}}{3.35 \times 10^{-24}\,\text{kg ms}^{-1}} = 1.88 \times 10^{-10}\,\text{m} \checkmark = 2.0 \times 10^{-10}\,\text{m (2 sf)} \checkmark$$

ⓔ (A/B grade) To get the final mark you have to show some valid working. You cannot get the mark if you just write down the numerical answer.

(c) The momentum of the electrons, p, is the same as the momentum of the neutrons but the mass of the electrons is much smaller than the mass of the neutrons. ✓

The kinetic energy is given by $p^2/2m$ so the kinetic energy of electron must be much higher. ✓

ⓔ (C grade) An alternative answer for the second mark is: If the speed of the electrons is much faster than the neutrons, and because their kinetic energy $E_k = \frac{1}{2}mv^2$, then the kinetic energy of the electrons is significantly higher because v^2 is more significant than m.

Question 5

Figure 4 shows part of an electron deflection tube in which a narrow beam of electrons is fired into the space between two parallel plate electrodes, X and Y. A constant potential difference, V, is applied between the two plates and the beam is observed to curve downwards towards plate Y.

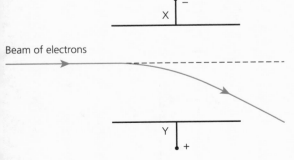

Figure 4

Questions & Answers

(a) The beam of electrons curves downwards towards plate Y at an increasing angle to its initial direction of travel. Explain why this happens. (3 marks)

(b) A student then applies a uniform magnetic field, of flux density B, at right angles to both the beam of electrons and the electric field between the plates X and Y. This effect causes an increase in the downward deflection of the beam.

 (i) The student then uses this arrangement to calculate the speed of the electrons in the beam. Describe the adjustments that the student needs to make to the flux density of the magnetic field to return the beam of electrons to its original direction. (1 mark)

 (ii) The potential difference between plates X and Y is V, and d is the perpendicular distance between the plates. If the speed of the electrons in the beam is $v = V/Bd$, the electrons travel through the two fields without being deflected. Explain why this happens. (2 marks)

(c) A heated metal filament cathode produces the beam of electrons by thermionic emission. If the student measured the potential difference between the anode and the filament cathode to be 4200 V, and she measured the speed of the electrons in the beam to be $3.9 \times 10^7 \, \text{m s}^{-1}$, calculate the specific charge on an electron. (3 marks)

Answer

(a) The force on the electron due to the electric field acts (vertically) downwards. ✓

This increases the vertical (component) of the velocity of each electron. ✓

The horizontal component of the velocity is unchanged (so the angle to the initial direction of motion of the electrons increases). ✓

ⓔ (A/B grade) Remember that motion perpendicular to a force is unaffected.

(b) (i) The student needs to reverse the direction of the magnetic flux density and adjust its strength slowly until the beam moves across the tube undeflected. ✓

 (ii) The force due to the magnetic field is given by $F = Bev$ and the force due to the electric field is given by $F = eV/d$. ✓
 Equating the two gives $Bev = eV/d$ and hence $v = V/Bd$ ✓

ⓔ (C grade) The symbols Q, q or e can be used to represent the charge on the electron.

(c) The amount of kinetic energy gained by the electrons is equal to the work done by the anode potential difference on the electrons, $\frac{1}{2}mv^2 = eV$ ✓

$$\frac{e}{m}\left(=\frac{v^2}{2V}\right) = \frac{(3.9 \times 10^7 \, \text{m s}^{-1})^2}{2 \times 4200 \, \text{V}} \checkmark = 1.8 \times 10^{11} \, \text{C kg}^{-1} \checkmark$$

ⓔ (C grade) Make sure that you calculate the values from the data given in the question, not from the data booklet.

Question 6

a) Using a suitable labelled diagram, describe a plane-polarised electromagnetic wave travelling through a vacuum in terms of electric fields and magnetic fields. (3 marks)

b) In 1864, James Clerk Maxwell published his theory of electromagnetic waves. In this he stated that the speed of all electromagnetic waves travelling through free space (like a vacuum) is given by:

$$c = \frac{1}{\sqrt{\mu_0 \varepsilon_0}}$$

where ε_0 is the permittivity of free space and μ_0 is the permeability of free space. Explain why Maxwell used this equation to show that light waves are part of the electromagnetic spectrum. (2 marks)

c) Figure 5 shows a simplified version of the apparatus used by Heinrich Hertz in 1887 to produce and detect radio waves. The aerial of the radio transmitter, T, and the metal loop of the detector, D, are in the same vertical plane.

Figure 5

(i) The transmitter aerial and the detector loop are in the positions shown in Figure 5. Explain why an alternating EMF is induced in the loop. (3 marks)

(ii) The detector loop is now rotated through 90° about the axis XY. Explain why the alternating EMF falls to zero in this new position. (1 mark)

Answer

(a)

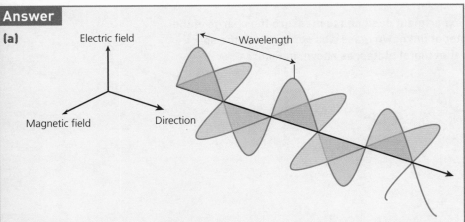

Diagram to show vibrations of an electric wave and a magnetic wave that are:

- perpendicular to each other ✓
- perpendicular to the direction of propagation of the waves ✓
- in phase ✓

Questions & Answers

@ (C grade) Remember that 3 marks means three separate points.

> **(b)** Any two of:
> The values of μ_0 and ε_0 can be determined experimentally. ✓ The values can then be substituted into Maxwell's equation, and this gives a value of the speed $c = 3.0 \times 10^8\,\text{m s}^{-1}$. ✓ This is the same value as the speed of light. ✓

@ (C grade) To get full marks, you need to compare the value determined in the calculation to the given value of c.

> **(c) (i)** The vibrations of the magnetic wave are perpendicular to the (plane of the) loop. ✓
> This causes an alternating magnetic flux linkage to the loop. ✓
> The alternating magnetic flux induces an alternating EMF in the loop. ✓

@ (C grade) There is an alternative explanation in terms of the electric-wave vibration: The electric-wave vibrations are parallel to the loop; ✓ this electric wave induces an EMF in the wire of the loop. ✓ Because the electric wave alternates, so does the induced EMF. ✓

> **(c) (ii)** There is now no magnetic flux linkage to the loop because it is parallel to the vibrations of the magnetic wave. This means that there is no induced EMF. ✓

@ (C grade) The alternative explanation using the electric wave involves stating that the electric field is now perpendicular to the plane of the loop so no EMF is induced.

Question 7

During a Millikan's oil drop experiment designed to measure the charge of the electron, a charged oil droplet of unknown mass was sprayed into the space between two horizontal parallel metal plates, as shown in Figure 6.

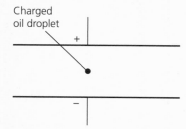

Figure 6

(a) The PD between the plates was set to zero and the charged droplet fell vertically at its terminal velocity.

   (i) Taking into consideration the forces acting on the droplet when it is falling at its terminal velocity, v, show that the radius, r, of the droplet is given by:

$$r = \left(\frac{9\eta v}{2\rho g} \right)^{\frac{1}{2}}$$

where η is the viscosity of air and ρ is the density of the oil droplet. (2 marks)

(ii) Explain how it is possible to use the radius of the oil droplet to determine its mass. (1 mark)

b) In the example shown in Figure 6, the separation between the two horizontal parallel metal plates was 6.0 mm and the droplet had a mass of 6.7×10^{-15} kg. The droplet was held stationary when the plate PD was 821 V.

(i) Calculate the charge of the oil droplet, expressing your answer to an appropriate number of significant figures (3 marks)

(ii) Robert Millikan was the first person to make accurate measurements of the charge carried by charged oil droplets. Outline the conclusions that Millikan made from these measurements. (2 marks)

Answer

(a) (i) When travelling at its terminal velocity, the resultant force on the droplet must be zero, and so the viscous force on the droplet equals its weight. ✓

The viscous force $= 6\pi\eta rv$ and the weight ($= mg$) $= 4\pi r^3 \rho g/3$.

$4\pi r^3 \rho g/3 = 6\pi\eta rv$ ✓ which rearranged gives: $r = \left(\frac{9\eta v}{2\rho g} \right)^{\frac{1}{2}}$

(ii) The equation $r = \left(\frac{9\eta v}{2\rho g} \right)^{\frac{1}{2}}$ can be used to calculate r, which can then be substituted into the formula $m = 4\pi r^3 \rho/3$ to find the mass of the droplet. ✓

⊕ (A/B grade) Alternatively, using $6\pi\eta rv = mg$, this can be rearranged to give $m = 6\pi\eta rv/g$.

(b) (i) The droplet weight = the electric force ✓

⊕ (E grade) You could also state: $mg = QV/d$

$Q = \dfrac{mgd}{V} = \dfrac{6.7 \times 10^{-15}\,\text{kg} \times 9.8\,\text{ms}^{-2} \times 6.0 \times 10^{-3}\,\text{m}}{821\,\text{V}} = 4.8 \times 10^{-19}\,\text{C}$ ✓

Answer to 2 sf. ✓

(b) (ii) Any two of the following:
- Each droplet has a charge that is a whole number $\times 1.6 \times 10^{-19}$ C. ✓

⊕ (E grade) Alternatively, each droplet has a charge that is a multiple number of the charge of the electron. ✓

- The minimum charge on each droplet (or the quantum of charge) is equal to the charge of the electron.
- The quantum of charge is equal to 1.6×10^{-19} C. ✓

Question 8

The tubes used in neon signs contain low-pressure neon gas, as shown in Figure 7. The neon gas inside the tube will conduct and emit light if a suitably high potential difference is applied across the two metal electrodes inside the tube.

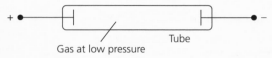

Figure 7

(a) (i) Describe the process by which the charged neon particles responsible for the conduction within the tube are produced. (2 marks)

(ii) When neon behaves like this it emits a spectrum of colours, but in particular a bright red light. Explain why the neon emits light and why it must be at low pressure. (3 marks)

(b) Explain why the specific charge of the ions inside the tube depends on the type of gas in the tube. (2 marks)

Answer

(a) (i) Electrons can be removed from the neon gas atoms forming positive neon ions. ✓

Electrical conduction occurs due to the movement of the freed electrons and the positive neon ions. ✓

(ii) Any three of:
- The neon ions and electrons have opposite charges and move in opposite directions. They collide with each other and emit photons of light as they recombine. ✓
- The electrons collide with neon gas atoms and cause excitation of electrons within the energy levels of the neon atoms. Photons of light are then emitted when the electrons undergo de-excitation. ✓
- The neon gas atoms need to be at low pressure so that they are far apart, ✓ otherwise the positive ions and the electrons would be stopped by other neon gas atoms. ✓

(b) The specific charge of the ions = charge of ion/mass of ion.

The charge of the ion does not depend on the type of gas, ✓ but the mass of the ion does depend on the type of gas. ✓

ⓔ (C grade) The specific charge of the ions could be stated in symbols: Q/m.

Question 9

9 The image of a thin sample under a transmission electron microscope (TEM) is formed by magnetic lenses that focus a beam of electrons as they pass through the sample.

   (i) When a magnetic lens deflects a beam of electrons it does so without changing the kinetic energy of the electrons in the beam. Explain how this happens.   (2 marks)

   (ii) A TEM has an anode potential of 21 kV. Calculate the de Broglie wavelength of the electrons in the beam in metres, giving your answer to a suitable number of significant figures.   (3 marks)

b) During the operation of a TEM the electron beam passes through a thin sample and a magnified image of the sample is formed on a fluorescent screen. Describe what happens to the electrons as they move between the sample and the screen. Your answer should include reference to the relevant wave–particle duality of electrons in relation to:

- the sample
- the deflection and focusing of the electron beam
- the screen
- the magnification and the quality of the image.

   You will be assessed on the quality of your written communication in this answer. (6 marks)

Answer

a) (i) The kinetic energy is constant because the magnetic force that acts on a moving electron is always perpendicular to its velocity (or direction of motion). ✓ This means that no work is done on the electron by the magnetic field. ✓

⊙ (C grade) For the second mark you must state that there is no acceleration in the direction of motion.

a) (ii) $$\lambda = \frac{h}{\sqrt{2meV}} = \frac{6.63 \times 10^{-34}\,\text{Js}}{\sqrt{2 \times 9.11 \times 10^{-31}\,\text{kg} \times 1.60 \times 10^{-19}\,\text{C} \times 21000\,\text{V}}} \quad ✓$$

$$= 8.5 \times 10^{-12}\,\text{m} \;✓ \text{ must have 2 sf } ✓$$

⊙ (A/B grade) You can get the significant-figure mark only if your answer shows some correct working. Due to rounding, you could have any numerical value from 8.5 to 8.6 to any number of significant figures (but not get the significant-figure mark).

⊙ The marks awarded for part (b) are determined by the quality of your written communication in addition to the standard of your scientific responses. Your answer is marked on a 'best-fit' basis assigning it to one of three levels using the criteria in the table on page 72.

(A–E grade) Your handwriting should be legible (the examiner must be able to read it) and the spelling, punctuation and grammar should be good enough for the meaning of your answer to be clear. Your answer will be assessed holistically — this means that the examiner will read the answer completely first and then assign a mark based on the whole of your response.

0 marks	Level 1 (E grade) (1–2 marks)	Level 2 (C grade) (3–4 marks)	Level 3 (A grade) (5–6 marks)
No relevant content	Lower level (poor to limited): 1 or 2 marks. Your answer has included a wave property and/or a particle property of electrons that is relevant to the context of the TEM, but it may not include where in the instrument they are relevant. Your answer may use incorrect terms (such as interference and refraction) and it may lack coherence and contain significant errors in terms of spelling and punctuation.	Intermediate level (modest to adequate): 3 or 4 marks. Your answer gives a logical and coherent description of some of the physical processes that occur and includes a relevant wave property or a relevant particle property. You have also included a description of why and where in the instrument each of these properties is relevant to the formation and quality of the image but your explanation of why each property is relevant is sketchy. Your answer is adequately or well-presented in terms of spelling, punctuation and grammar.	High level (good to excellent): 5 or 6 marks. Your answer gives a comprehensive and logical description of most of the physical processes that occur and you have recognised at least two relevant properties of electrons, including a relevant wave property and a relevant particle property. You have also included a description of why and where in the instrument each of these properties is relevant to the formation and quality of the image. Your answer is well-presented in terms of spelling, punctuation and grammar.

A good answer should include most of the following physics ideas:

At the sample

Scattering and/or diffraction by structures in the sample affect the electrons as they pass through the sample — this is a wave property.

At the magnetic lenses

- The electrons are deflected by magnetic lenses — this is a particle property.
- The first (condenser) lens forms the electrons into a parallel beam directed at the sample.
- The second (objective) lens deflects and focuses the electron beam to form an (intermediate) image.
- The third (magnifier) lens deflects and focuses the beam of electrons onto the screen.

At the screen

- Collisions between the electrons and the atoms of the screen cause excitation of the atoms — this is a particle property.
- Photons are emitted by the excited atoms allowing the image to be seen.

The image quality

- Is affected by the loss of kinetic energy (or velocity or increase in the de Broglie wavelength) of the electrons as they pass through the sample, which in turn affects the deflection/focusing by the magnetic lenses — this is a particle property.

Electrons passing through the sample can repeatedly scatter or diffract within the sample if it is too thick — this is a wave property.

The beam of electrons can diffract as it passes through each lens — this is a wave property.

Diffraction can affect the resolution of nearby image points on the screen — this is a wave property.

Point objects that are too close or overlap cannot be resolved — this is a wave property.

Question 10

) One of Einstein's two postulates in his theory of special relativity stated that the speed of light in free space, c, is invariant. Explain what this statement means. (1 mark)

) A particle accelerator injects a beam of identical particles into a long, straight vacuum tube at a speed of $0.98c$. The particles are detected when they pass between two detectors 25 m apart. The particles in the beam are unstable and they decay, causing the intensity of the beam to decrease between the two detectors. The intensity detected by the second detector is found to be a quarter of the intensity detected by the first detector. Calculate the half-life of the particles in their rest frame. (4 marks)

) As the speed of the particles increases towards the speed of light, their mass increases. Calculate the speed of the particles at which their mass is twice their rest mass. (2 marks)

) Make a copy of the axes shown in Figure 8. On your copy, sketch a graph to show how the mass, m, of a particle changes from its rest mass m_0 as its speed v increases from zero up to c. On your graph, label the point Q where the mass of the particle is twice its rest mass. (3 marks)

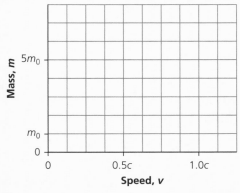

Figure 8

) Einstein's theory of special relativity does not allow matter particles to travel at the speed of light. Explain why this is the case by considering the relationship between the energy of a particle and its mass, and the shape of the graph you have drawn in part (d). (2 marks)

Answer

(a) The speed of light, c, is the same regardless of the speed of the light source or the observer. ✓

ⓔ (C grade) An answer stating that the speed of light is the same in all frames of reference is insufficient to score the mark.

(b) The distance between the two detectors in the rest frame of reference of the particles is given by $l = 25\text{m} \times \sqrt{\left(1 - (0.98c)^2 / c^2\right)} = 5.0\,\text{years}$ ✓

The time taken for the particles to cover this distance in their rest frame is:

$$\left(= \frac{\text{distance}}{\text{speed}} = \frac{5.0\text{m}}{0.98c\,\text{ms}^{-1}} \right) = 1.7 \times 10^{-8}\,\text{s} \checkmark$$

The time taken for this journey must be two half-lives because the intensity drops by ¼. ✓

So the half-life of the particles is $\left(\dfrac{1.7 \times 10^{-8}\,\text{s}}{2} \right) = 8.5 \times 10^{-9}\,\text{s}$ ✓

ⓔ (A/B grade) An alternative way of answering this question is to consider the time taken in the rest frame of the detectors:

$$\left(\frac{\text{distance}}{\text{speed}} = \frac{25.0\text{m}}{0.98c\,\text{ms}^{-1}} \right) = 8.5 \times 10^{-8}\,\text{s} \checkmark$$

Then the time taken in the rest frame of the particles is given by:

$8.5 \times 10^{-8}\,\text{s} \times \sqrt{\left(1 - (0.98c)^2 / c^2\right)}$ ✓ $= 1.7 \times 10^{-8}\,\text{s}$ ✓

and then complete to find the half-life.

(c) Using: $m = \dfrac{m_0}{\sqrt{1 - \dfrac{v^2}{c^2}}}$ gives $2 = \dfrac{1}{\sqrt{1 - \dfrac{v^2}{c^2}}} \Rightarrow 0.5 = \sqrt{1 - \dfrac{v^2}{c^2}}$ ✓

Rearranging this equation gives: $v = \sqrt{1 - 0.5^2}\,c = 0.866c = 2.6 \times 10^8\,\text{ms}^{-1}$ ✓

ⓔ You could write your answer in either format.

(d) The graph is a curve starting at $v = 0$ and $m = m_0$ and rises smoothly. ✓

The curve should pass through $2m_0$ at $v = 0.87c$. ✓

The curve is asymptotic to $v = c$ (and it should not cross or touch $v = c$ or curve back towards the y-axis). ✓

(d) (A/B grade) The second mark is an example of error carried forward from the speed calculated in part (c), provided you plotted it accurately. For the third mark you must have a visible white space between the curve and the $v = c$ line; *and* the curve must reach at least $7m_0$.

(e) The energy of a particle is given by $E = mc^2$, so (as v tends towards c) the energy of the particle increases as its mass increases. ✓

The mass tends towards infinity as v approaches c, so its energy tends towards infinity, which is (physically) impossible. ✓

(f) Or for 1 mark only: Using Newton's second law, $F = ma$, the force acting on the particle increases as the mass increases. Because the mass tends towards infinity as v tends to c, the force tends towards infinity, which is (physically) impossible ✓

(C grade) Alternatively (but only scores 1 mark) — the mass of the particle would be infinite at $v = c$ which is (physically) impossible. ✓

Knowledge check answers

Knowledge check answers

1 $M = \dfrac{f_o}{f_e} = \dfrac{120 \times 10^{-2}\,m}{15 \times 10^{-3}\,m} = 80$

2 a Spherical aberration is the blurring of an image due to rays of light from the edge of a lens or mirror not passing through the same focal point as the rest of the rays.

 b Chromatic aberration is the blurring of an image in a refracting telescope due to the different colours of light refracting by different angles through the lens and passing through different focal points.

3 Mirrors reflect different colours of light equally. Lenses refract different colours through different angles forming a blurred image.

4 $\theta \approx \dfrac{\lambda}{D} \approx \dfrac{620 \times 10^{-9}\,m}{32 \times 10^{-2}\,m} \approx 1.94 \times 10^{-6}\,radians$

5 This is expressed as a percentage of the incoming absorbed photons that are converted into electrons per second.

6 The Earth's atmosphere absorbs most UV radiation, so UV telescopes need to be space-based. There is a small IR 'window' in the atmosphere so some IR telescopes can be situated on the top of high mountains, but others are space-based. There is a wide radio 'window' throughout the atmosphere, and because the wavelengths of radio waves are long, nearly all radio telescopes are Earth-based.

7 The star with the lowest apparent magnitude, Betelgeuse, is brightest. The difference in apparent magnitude is $(2.0 - 0.4) = 1.6$. The difference in brightness is therefore $(2.51)^{1.6} = 4.4$ (2 sf).

8 a $\dfrac{4.24ly \times 9.46 \times 10^{15}\,m}{1.50 \times 10^{11}\,m} = 2.67 \times 10^{5}\,AU$

 b $\dfrac{4.24ly}{3.26ly} = 1.30pc$

9 $m - M = 5\log_{10}\left(\dfrac{d}{10}\right) \Rightarrow M = m - 5\log_{10}\left(\dfrac{d}{10}\right)$

$= 5.357 - 5\log_{10}\left(\dfrac{1.30\,pc}{10}\right) = 9.79$

10 Luminosity $= \sigma A T^4 = 5.7 \times 10^{-8} \times 4\pi \times$

$(696000 \times 10^8)^2 \times (5778K)^4 = 3.9 \times 10^{26}\,W$ (2 sf)

$\lambda_{max}T = 2.9 \times 10^{-3}\,m\,K \Rightarrow \lambda_{max} = \dfrac{2.9 \times 10^{-3}\,m\,K}{5778\,K}$

$= 5.0 \times 10^{-7}\,m$ (2 sf)

11 The absorption spectrum of the Sun is the sequence of dark absorption lines in the continuous spectrum emitted by the Sun, corresponding to particular elements at a temperature of 5778 K.

12 If the Sun-like main sequence star has a luminosity equal to 1 and a surface temperature of about 5500 K, the corresponding red dwarf will have a luminosity about 1000 times higher, but a surface temperature of about 3500 K. The white dwarf formed from the red giant will be about 100 times less luminous than the main sequence star, but will have a surface temperature of 11 000 K.

13 $R_S = \dfrac{2GM}{c^2}$

$= \dfrac{2 \times 6.67 \times 10^{-11}\,Nm^2kg^{-2} \times 1.5 \times 10^{31}\,kg}{\left(3.0 \times 10^8\,ms^{-1}\right)^2}$

$= 22233m = 22km$ (2 sf)

14 Type 1a supernovae occur in binary star systems involving a white dwarf and (commonly) a red giant. Matter from the expanding red dwarf is pulled towards the white dwarf. When its mass reaches about 1.4 solar masses, the white dwarf collapses reigniting thermonuclear reactions within the white dwarf triggering a type 1a supernova explosion.

15 Cosmological redshift is the apparent increase in wavelength of the radiation emitted by a star or galaxy moving away from Earth due to the expansion of the Universe.

16 Quasars are some of the oldest objects in the Universe, formed soon after the Big Bang. As a result they are some of the furthest objects away from Earth, travelling at the highest recessional velocities, hence they have the highest z-parameters because $z \propto v$.

17 $v = Hd \Rightarrow d = \dfrac{v}{H} = \dfrac{1320km\,s^{-1}}{65kms^{-1}Mpc^{-1}} = 20.(3)Mpc$

18 Cosmological redshift; cosmological microwave background radiation; 75% : 25% stellar proportion of H : He.

19 $t = \dfrac{1}{H} \Rightarrow H = \dfrac{1}{t} = \dfrac{1}{13.8 \times 10^9\,y} = 7.25 \times 10^{-11}\,y^{-1}$

20 The spectral line will be alternately blue-shifted and red-shifted as the star orbits around its common centre of gravity with the exoplanet. This will cause an increase and then a decrease in the wavelength of the spectral line as observed from Earth.

21 $\dfrac{1}{2}mv^2 = eV \Rightarrow v = \sqrt{\dfrac{2eV}{m}}$

$= \sqrt{\dfrac{2 \times 1.6 \times 10^{-19}\,C \times 4500V}{9.11 \times 10^{-31}\,kg}} = 4.0 \times 10^7\,ms^{-1}$

$$\frac{e}{m} = \frac{V}{B^2 rd}$$

$$= \frac{11.5\,\text{V}}{\left(0.35 \times 10^{-3}\,\text{T}\right)^2 \times 22 \times 10^{-3}\,\text{m} \times 25 \times 10^{-3}\,\text{m}}$$

$$= 1.7 \times 10^{11}\,\text{Ckg}^{-1}$$

Thomson's experiment only measured the e/m ratio. Thomson did not have a value for the mass of the electron.

$$\frac{QV}{d} = mg \Rightarrow Q = \frac{mgd}{V}$$

$$= \frac{1.3 \times 10^{-15}\,\text{kg} \times 9.8\,\text{Nkg}^{-1} \times 25 \times 10^{-3}\,\text{m}}{1000\,\text{V}} =$$

$$= 3.19 \times 10^{-19}\,\text{C}$$

If $e = 1.6 \times 10^{-19}\,\text{C}$, then $n = \dfrac{3.19 \times 10^{-19}\,\text{C}}{1.6 \times 10^{-19}\,\text{C}} \approx 2$

Millikan realised that the drops would have different charges, and that the overall charge on each drop would be an integer number of the charge on the electron, e. By measuring enough charges he was able to find pairs of drops with a charge of ne and $(n + 1)e$, hence allowing him to determine e.

Newton proposed that light behaves as a particle. Huygens proposed that light behaves as a wave.

Only diffraction.

Newton's theory could not explain the diffraction effect in Young's experiment.

$$c = \frac{1}{\sqrt{\mu_0 \varepsilon_0}}$$

$$= \frac{1}{\sqrt{4\pi \times 10^{-7}\,\text{Hm}^{-1} \times 8.85 \times 10^{-12}\,\text{Fm}^{-1}}} =$$

$$= 2.998 \times 10^8\,\text{ms}^{-1} = \left(3.00 \times 10^8\,\text{ms}^{-1} \text{ to 3 sf}\right)$$

Fizeau's experimental measurement confirmed Maxwell's theoretical prediction.

Hertz set up a set of standing waves and measured the distance between adjacent antinodes. This distance is half of one wavelength.

The UV catastrophe is the observation that the energy emitted by a black body does not increase as the wavelength decreases into the UV spectrum.

33 The photoelectric effect is the emission of electrons from a metal surface when they interact with incident photons with energy greater than the work function of the metal.

34 $hf = E_{\text{kmax}} + \phi \Rightarrow E_{\text{kmax}} = hf - \phi = 2.7\,\text{eV} - 2.3\,\text{eV} = 0.4\,\text{eV}$

35 $\lambda = \dfrac{h}{p} = \dfrac{h}{mv} = \dfrac{6.6 \times 10^{-34}\,\text{J s}}{9.11 \times 10^{-31}\,\text{kg} \times 1.2 \times 10^8\,\text{ms}^{-1}}$

$$= 6.0 \times 10^{-12}\,\text{ms}^{-1}$$

36 Electrons are focused by magnetic fields generated by coiled electromagnets.

37 The tunnelling current between the tip and the surface is kept constant by the tip moving up and down by piezoelectric transducers as it scans across the surface. The surface is plotted by how much the tip moves up and down to keep the current constant at each point.

38 The æther was the medium proposed by Huygens for light waves to propagate through in space.

39 If the æther existed, rotating the interferometer through 90° should have produced a change in the interference pattern observed in the eyepiece. Michelson and Morley did not see any change in the pattern and so they suggested that the æther did not exist.

40 The two postulates of Einstein's theory of special relativity are: physical laws have the same form in all inertial frames; and the speed of light in free space is invariant.

41 Distance travelled $d = vt$, so during a half-life of 1.56 μs muons would travel $d = vt = 0.98 \times 3 \times 10^8\,\text{ms}^{-1} \times 1.56 \times 10^{-6}\,\text{s} = 459\,\text{m}$. During a half-life of 7.84 μs, the muons would travel $d = vt = 0.98 \times 3 \times 10^8\,\text{ms}^{-1} \times 7.84 \times 10^{-6}\,\text{s} = 2305\,\text{m}$.

42 $l = l_0\sqrt{1 - \dfrac{v^2}{c^2}} = 6.8\,\text{m} \times \sqrt{1 - \dfrac{(0.2c)^2}{c^2}} = 6.66\,\text{m}$

43 As the velocity of an object increases, the consequences are: the mass of the object increases (as measured by an observer); and it requires more energy to increase the velocity of the object.

Index

Note: **bold** page numbers indicate defined terms